BAUCHER AND THE ORDINARY HORSEMAN

Balance, Softness and Feel in Everyday Riding

Including a further conversation between God and the horse

Tom Widdicombe

ISBN 978-1-291-82456-8

CONTENTS

Foreword   4

1 The horse's mouth   5

2 Braces, resistances, softness and feel   23

3 More about the bit   32

4 Balance   42

5 How to sit on the horse   51

6 Weight-bearing posture, neck extension
                    and going forwards   57

7 Lifting the horse's head and neck   63

8 Is your horse straight?   75

9 Training your horse step-by-step   84

10 'Hand without legs, legs without hand'   90

11 Systems, teachers, horse-trainer speak, and you   93

A further conversation between God and the horse   100

Recommended reading   105

FOREWORD

Several years ago I wrote a book about horsemanship. I went out
of my way not to give advice on how to do anything. At the time I
thought it was a good idea, but now I realise the truth of the matter
was that I didn't really know anything worth advising anyone about
anyway.

In this book I am taking the opposite approach: it is full of advice,
and I am not shy about handing it out. There are some basic truths
about horses, how they move and how they best carry a rider that
I believe are universal. There will be other ways of getting to the
same place, but there is only one true place to get to. This book is
about a simple, straightforward way of training horses. It works, and
the horses are fine with it too.

I have the privilege of working with my wife Sarah, from whom I
learn most of my stuff, and our friend Kate, who is a talented rider.
Without Sarah and Kate there is no doubt that by now I'd definitely
be indoors watching the telly.

Note: Throughout this book, I refer to the rider or trainer
as a 'horseman'. This is purely to avoid the clumsy expression
'horseperson'.

1 THE HORSE'S MOUTH

I was never very keen on working with my horse in the school – I didn't see the point. We could get around fine, we went all over the place. We weren't too bothered by difficult terrain or by what other people were doing around us either. As far as I was concerned, the nearest I came to needing to school my horse was for opening and shutting gates, and I pretty much did that when I got to them. And if it was too difficult I just got off, manoeuvred us through the gate, and got back on.

So what changed? Well, a couple of things really. One day several years ago I was sitting on my horse, Splash, arguing with my wife about why she was interested in riding around in circles and not going anywhere. She just said to me quite simply, 'Well ok then, let's see you ride around in a small circle in each direction.' I laughed and thought to myself, 'Just how hard can this be?' I set off to go to the right, and when I put a small touch on my right-hand rein my horse followed it easily around the circle. Then I changed the touch from the right rein to the left rein – and that was the exact moment when I realised I had a bit of a job on my hands. Splash felt the feel in the rein change from right to left, and instead of simply walking around the circle to her left she kind of lurched towards the middle of the circle through her shoulder. To me it felt as if she was losing her balance and falling sideways.

'That's weird,' I said, 'I'll try that again.' But no matter how hard I tried to get her to just follow the feel in the rein around the circle, she couldn't do it – she kept falling sideways. So then I started doing things that I have always considered to be extra to what I should be doing: I tried to block her with the outside rein, I tried to hold her up with my inside leg, and I tried adjusting my balance to one side and then the other. Nothing was working for me and I was sitting on my horse having a bit of a meltdown about the future of my riding. 'Oh my, this could take some sorting out,' I said to myself.

The horse's mouth

And that was the start of it. For years I had ridden my horse around no problem, and on that day I had a glimpse of the future. If only I hadn't seen that — life could have been so simple.

Around the same time that I was starting work on the steering issues I was having with Splash, my wife Sarah had a little horse up here called Molly. We had actually bred her ten years earlier and sold her on as a three-year-old. One way and another she had come a bit unstuck, and she ended up back with us for a while to see if we could help her along a bit.

It's quite difficult to explain what was wrong with Molly — some people thought she was fine. She tried really hard and she did make an attempt at everything you asked her to do, but somehow or other she was always mentally absent. In her mind, she was still in the field with her mates. It felt as if you were riding a horse that wasn't there. Most of the time it was quite safe — it showed up in things like circles becoming ovals towards the gate end of the school, and speeding up a little to try to get past you when you led her back to the field. But occasionally it was quite dangerous, with things like crazy rushing and suddenly refusing to go near things or to certain places.

So, because Sarah and I are the way we are, we needed to get this sorted out for Molly and it became a bit of a mission for us. That summer we spent hours and hours trying everything we knew to help get that little horse's mind away from her friends in the field and back into her body. Many times we were out there working as darkness fell, desperately trying to get anything, the tiniest positive thing, for Molly to take back with her to the field that night.

At first we were working with Molly as a paid job, and over the first couple of weeks we had actually made good progress. But as she settled into the herd here, fairly quickly the wheels fell off and we were pretty much back to square one. After a few more weeks of getting not very far at all, we decided that we couldn't take any more money for what amounted to nearly nothing in return, and so we asked the owner if we could have Molly here as our own project. Our offer was accepted.

We learned a lot working with that little horse. We certainly learned that most of what we knew at that time and most of what we did wasn't ever going to work. But far and away the most important thing we learned was the one thing that really made the difference. Looking back, I can see that if Molly walked into our yard today we would have done that job in a very different way.

Now, I'm not one for believing in the 'magic bullet' approach to horse training – I've seen too many of them to think that the next idea that comes along is going to be the answer to everything. It's always a tempting thought, though, isn't it? And it was a bit like that with Molly.

We'd recently come across the work of the French horse trainer François Baucher. He was a prolific writer and his methods caused much discussion in early nineteenth-century equestrian circles. His life and times are well documented, and I enjoyed reading about them. Baucher worked in a circus in Paris and in those days circus entertainment was in the main centred around horses and the ridden performances that people could present with them. There is a fabulous story about a beautiful but impossible horse called Gericault. His owner offered him as a gift to the first person who could ride him around the Bois de Boulogne. One of Baucher's students took on the challenge, succeeded, won the horse and promptly gave him to Baucher as a gift. Three weeks later the circus was packed as Baucher made his first public appearance riding Gericault. The crowd was stunned to silence by the progress he had made and the quality of his performance.

One of the first things we picked up from Baucher was the need for the horse to have a soft, mobile mouth. The information that we were getting about Baucher was coming from a little book called *Racinet Explains Baucher*, and one morning when I took my wife her morning cup of tea she simply said, 'Listen to this quote, it's amazing:

The horse's mouth

"*The big discovery one makes when one starts studying and applying Baucherist techniques is that once light in hand, that is, relaxed and mobile in his lower jaw, a horse becomes disciplined.*'"

'Mmmm, might be worth a try,' I replied.

Spurred on by the information I had from Racinet's book but with not too much idea about what I was doing, I began to look more closely at the relationship that our horses had with the bit. That in turn made me look at my relationship with the bit and what I understood about it.

In view of Splash's difficulty in turning left, I stood in front of my horse, got her front feet levelled up, put my hands on either side of her face and gently held the bit rings on each side of her mouth. I lifted her head and neck until the poll was the highest point and then I tried to turn her head first to the right, which she did fine, and then to the left, which she couldn't do at all. First she resisted my request and then, as I gently continued asking, rather than give me the bend I was looking for she kept trying to move her whole front end to the left. It felt as if she wanted to fall that way. The penny dropped for me at that moment, or should I say that all sorts of pennies were dropping all over the place. I suddenly realised that *I could feel the whole horse in my hands*, and that maybe through that I would be able to help sort out all the misunderstandings that were going on between us.

Later that day Sarah and I were in the school working through a few ideas we'd had that we hoped might help Molly. Things weren't going that well and we could both see another marathon session stretching before us. I decided to see how things felt in Molly's mouth. One thing we knew for sure about Molly was that she would drop back behind the bit. I'll just explain what I mean by this: put simply, if a horse is 'behind the bit' they will not accept pressure, however light, from the bit and in order to avoid that pressure they come back off it. Actually, we'd taught Molly to do that ourselves. At that time, when we picked up the reins we liked our horses to give at the poll by tucking their nose. It's a cowboy thing – you can find

8

it in a lot of western training books and also if you watch western trainers and riders.

So, I put my hands on the bit rings and gently held the bit on either side of Molly's mouth – no pressure, just holding it to see what was going on in there. What I felt was shocking. That little horse's whole mouth was twitching and fidgeting. She desperately wanted to get behind the bit, in fact she wanted anything except just to be still and relax with it. She really didn't want to feel my hands on that bit at all. I hung in there because I felt it would be wrong not to make some effort to help Molly find a way of settling down and being happy with the bit just sitting there softly in her mouth. It was some minutes before she gradually started to relax and realise that my hands holding the bit were not a threat to her, and that things were actually going to be all right. In retrospect, I can see that it is hardly surprising that Molly felt so uncomfortable with what I was doing. After years of believing that the correct thing to do was move away from the bit, suddenly she was being asked to relax and be with it.

So that is the beginning of a story that has come on a long way. I have progressed from a humble and slightly nervous beginning to a point where I am now certain about what I am doing. I know without doubt that my horse has to trust and 100% accept that the bit and the person controlling it are consistent and reliable. For my horse to understand that, I also have to understand it. It is not possible to teach a horse correctly something that you don't understand yourself. From here you can go on to build things up with your horse. It's not a five-minute job, that's for sure. There are many, many steps along the way, and in this book we are going to go through all of them in a way that I hope will be simple and clear for anyone who wants to follow them. This is a practical book about horsemanship. I am going to try to write it for ordinary riders like me, who don't necessarily want anything more than a nice horse to ride around the place. But remember, if you do want to do more with your horse, and there is nothing wrong in that, then it is even more important that you put the correct basics and understanding into your horse (and yourself).

Before we go any further with this, I just want to mention a few basic points about how to be with horses. There are some very simple, practical things that need to be in place in order for your horse to be relaxed and happy around you. As I write this I am thinking, 'Uh oh, this subject is a book in itself, and I really don't want to write that particular book right now.' So I'll try to keep it brief. Just remember: you need to get this part of your horsemanship really well sorted, or the rest of it isn't going to make much sense at all.

- You need to sort out your boundaries and your personal space, and that you move your horse – your horse doesn't move you.
- You need to be able to work with your horse in a non-emotional way.
- You need to understand that the horse has no hidden agenda – he is only interested in self-preservation and an easy life. Your horse definitely does not look at life through human eyes.
- You need to show your horse absolutely that you are not a threat to him, and that you are not going to put him in danger.

For the human, all of the above is a way of being, not some kind of intellectual understanding or a whimsical choice of how you'd like things to be.

If you don't understand any of the above, or are struggling to put it into practice, then you need to find yourself a good horseman to work alongside until you get it, and you feel yourself naturally presenting yourself to the horse in a way that includes everything described above. The reason I say this is because the best, if not the only, way to learn this is to watch someone over a period of time to whom this comes naturally – watch and learn from them, and practise until it becomes natural to you too.

Let's talk a little more about the horse's mouth. I know some people get quite upset about putting a bit in a horse's mouth, and that is of course up to them. I personally don't have a problem with using a bit. In fact, I see huge advantages. I can also see that there could be some huge disadvantages for the horse if the bit is used in a bad way, for example, with force or restraint. So let's get this straight – it's not the bit, it's what you do with it that makes it good or bad.

I have seen horses that are really struggling with having a bit in their mouth, but after a few minutes of careful explanation to them about how it works and what it means, they really settle down and become very happy indeed with the situation. At the point where I realised the power of explanation in working with horses, it fundamentally changed my view of horse training. Now I look at everything I ask my horse to do from the point of view of 'Does my horse understand what I am asking him to do?' Without exception, making sure that he understands what is going on is the key to having a peaceful horse.

When you gently hold the bit with your hands on either side of the horse's mouth, you will feel every little reaction in him to what is going on. If you move the bit in any direction you will feel whether the horse is happy to go with it, or slightly reluctant, or even violently against the idea. I'm guessing that everyone accepts that it is obviously best if the horse is happy to follow the bit wherever you take it.

After doing this with a few different horses, I worked out that a really good way of helping a horse that is worried by the bit is to make sure that it moves as little as possible within the horse's mouth. If the bit sits there quietly, the horse begins to trust that it

The horse's mouth

is safe and that it isn't going to suddenly move in some way that is completely irrational. Imagine, if you will, having a lump of metal in your mouth over which you have no control and that might, at any moment, move in any direction and at any speed. On top of that, you have no idea what causes the irrational movements by which you are threatened. This, my friends, is the situation in which very many horses find themselves. And that situation is precisely why so many horses have developed so many different techniques and strategies for defending themselves against the bit.

Many years ago – I would have been about 40 at the time – one of my friends arranged for a group of us to go out for a trek on the moor. The outing was to be my friend's birthday treat, given to him by his wife. I arrived at the yard and joined the group of about ten. The yard owner came striding out of the barn and went through a few safety precautions; she then asked if any of us had ridden before. I put up my hand, along with a couple of the others. We were given horses that required more experience than the complete beginners in the group.

It turned out that I was to ride a ten-year-old thoroughbred mare called Touch and Go. To this day, I have never enjoyed riding a horse as much as I enjoyed riding her. She truly lived up to her name, but in the most sensible way you could imagine. I was relatively new to horses – I'd say about three or four years into it at that point – and although I didn't know much in terms of technique or specifics, I did know how nice it was to gently ask the horse to stop, go or turn and have no resistance whatsoever to my request. Looking back, I can see that I was already searching for how things should be between me and the horse. Touch and Go was the first horse I had ever sat on that seemed to operate in sync with me rather than separately. It was a joy, and I have never forgotten that ride. I tried to buy her there and then, but the owner knew what she had and, unsurprisingly, she wasn't for sale.

Back working on the ground with Splash, once I had started to feel what was going on in her mouth while she was standing still, I decided it would be a good thing to see what happened when we moved along. So, standing in front of my horse and holding the bit on either side, I began to walk backwards, bringing her along with me (I knew Splash would not push through me, so this was quite safe). It didn't take her long to get the hang of that, so I tried a right turn and that went fine too. I tried to simulate the feel that Splash would get from the rein when I asked her for the turn while riding, by putting just a touch on the bit towards the corner of her mouth to get a little right bend in the neck. Yep, no problem, and around the corner we went. We travelled straight again, and then I tried the same thing to the left. 'Whoa, what the heck is going on there?' I thought to myself, as Splash lurched over onto her left shoulder. I could clearly feel that she had lost her balance and was still totally unable to walk around the line of the corner.

I tried the left turn a couple more times and began to feel that there was quite a resistance in Splash's neck when I asked for the left bend. She really, really didn't want to bend that way. I went back to getting the left bend with us both standing still until it was coming pretty nicely, and then tried it on the move one more time. As soon as I felt the resistance I became a little more persistent in my ask, and for a few steps there was a minor confrontation as I asked Splash to do something she clearly wasn't happy about. And then, just for a moment, she let it go and so found a release from my ask. A couple more times and she had the idea – and, as I would see it now, she *felt safe* about giving me that bend.

So now that my horse could give me that left-hand bend, she could also start to practise walking around a left turn without losing her balance. And from there it was only a short time until it was all working nicely with me riding her, too.

༄

Meanwhile, the job with Molly was taking us into even more new territory. We had already read quite a bit about the soft, mobile mouth originally put forward by Baucher, and well documented by several horsemen since. Sarah was working hard with Molly to

13

establish the soft mouth on cue. Now think about what this entails, for the horse. Think about what I said about that piece of metal in their mouth, and the crazy things many of them have to put up with there. Think about all the defences horses build in to cope with all this, and then someone comes along and says, 'No, it's OK, trust me, you can relax your mouth.' Add in all Molly's anxieties about wanting to be back up in the field with her mates and this was proving to be quite a job.

What you are asking for when you ask a horse to have a soft mouth on cue is actually *total trust*. Even so, one way and another we began to get a bit of a result and, unbelievably, Molly began to change. It was quite interesting for us, because it was as if we were watching her mind come back from the field and slowly take up residence inside herself, where it is supposed to be. The more we went on, the better things got and the softer the horse became.

So here is how to train a horse to offer a soft mouth on cue. Stand in front of your horse, facing him, and take hold of the bit on either side of his mouth (if you are worried about your horse trying to push into you, you will need to get some horsemanship basics in place first). If there are any resistances from him even to this – say, for example, pushing down on the bit or pulling back off it – just hold firm and wait for him to accept that it is safe for him to just stand there with you holding the bit softly in his mouth. When he is quiet and happy with that, gently lift the bit into the corners of his mouth in a movement towards his ears and keep it there until he begins to move his jaw – you may feel him relax even more with the situation at this point. When this happens, gently release the bit downwards away from the corners of his mouth and softly hold it in place in its normal position.

It won't be long before your horse learns that when he feels the bit move towards the corners of his mouth he can release his jaw. Soon he will start to kind of lick the bit and you will see (and feel) his tongue moving quietly in and out of his mouth. The plan is

14

that soon, when you are riding him, you will be able to ask him to release his jaw whenever you want him to, by gently using the reins to lift the bit.

Now let's look at a few details in this process. Firstly, it is important to make sure that the action of the bit is always towards the corners of the mouth. By doing this you avoid putting pressure on the horse's tongue which is, to say the very least, uncomfortable for him. There would never really be a time, one that I can think of anyway, when you would want to use the bit to put a lot of pressure on the tongue.

Secondly, let's look at what to do if your horse has learned to put pressure on the bit. I know that some people teach their horses to travel with weight on the bit, but for our purposes that is completely out. We are looking to train our horse to carry his own weight and that of the rider, and to be free from the physical brace and loss of balance that would be caused by leaning on the bit. So, when you pick up the bit in your hands, if you feel any lean from your horse you need to explain to him that this isn't what you are looking for. This explanation could range in difficulty from quite easy to near impossible, depending on how confirmed this behaviour has become.

As you feel the lean come into the bit, lift it higher until your horse carries the weight of his own head and neck himself – you should feel no weight at all in your hands. You may find that for now you have to work with the bit, and consequently your horse's head and neck, higher than you might imagine in order to avoid the lean. The aim is that as time goes on the work will become clear to the horse, the lean will disappear and horse can resume a lower position of his head and neck without also resuming the lean. If the lean is really confirmed and persistent, I am not averse to simply asking the horse to quit doing it by vibrating the bit up and down a little to show him that it's not a comfortable thing to lean on.

I'm going to say right here, I have worked with a few horses – generally older and almost always used for competition – where the

lean is so confirmed and so difficult for the horse to leave behind
that I have come away thinking, 'Nah, it's not worth it, and it's not
really very fair on the horse either, so maybe I should go and find
a younger horse – there are plenty of them out there.' But on the
whole, I'd say that you *can* get the job done so don't give up too
easily.

We are starting our work at the mouth, or more specifically at
the relationship between the bit, our hands and the horse's mouth.
If we can help the horse to relax his mouth and accept the bit,
then we can move on and help the rest of the horse to relax too.
Everything we do along the way is going to make perfect sense
to the horse, and we are not planning on moving on until we are
pretty sure that each part of the job is nicely in place. Our goal is
to help our horse to work freely, without tension, and in a way that
will keep him healthy both physically and mentally.

We had made a pretty encouraging start with Molly's mouth.
However, one day when we took her into the school there was a
huge pile of white plastic chairs dumped right where we wanted to
work. Molly was not at all sure about them, to the extent that she
felt the need to keep no less than 20 metres away. This could so
easily have been one of those situations where you could have an
endless discussion how best to sort it out – should we keep riding
around and as she gets more comfortable with the chairs try to
get closer to them? Or should we lead her up to investigate them?
Or….We have spent hours and hours over the years discussing this
kind of stuff. We have used all manner of little tricks and techniques
to sort out this and similar situations. And we have also discussed
not only the immediate success of any particular method, but
also the long-term effect of different methods on the relationship
between the rider and the horse.

But this time we tried something different: could we override
Molly's anxiety by using our newly built-in cue to relax her mouth?
So, every time Molly baulked at the chairs Sarah just asked her

16

to relax her jaw, and then when she did she quietly asked her to pass by closer to the chairs, until she baulked again, and then Sarah repeated the process. It took no time at all for Molly to reach the chairs and give them a thorough checking out with her nose, before proceeding as if they were no problem at all.

So, let's be clear here – I'm not saying that the soft mouth alone is the magic technique that solves all problems, but that little scenario did make us wonder if now we might at least have some kind of direct and effective say in the stress levels of our horse. We began to realize that the horse could see us as pretty useful in times of crisis. Of course, we had always strived for this kind of relationship anyway through the way we set up our basic interactions, but now we were beginning to see a whole new level of communication opening up between human and horse. On that day, we witnessed what I now see as the start of a total communication – a kind of system of oneness or unity between the rider and the horse. I have to admit, I was excited.

Thinking about the example of Molly and the chairs leads on to another very important concept in training horses. Our priority must always be to protect the horse's mental state. Inevitably there will be circumstances where our own priorities override that rule, and I have fallen into that hole many times. Unfortunately when that happens, from the horse's point of view, right there and then, he loses any faith that you have helped him build up in you.

Recently I worked very hard with a horse of mine that over the years I have had some difficulties with. Some days she was utterly brilliant, other days she was really nervous and jumpy. I spent several weeks working her in the indoor school, slowly building up the new way that I was training my horses. I got her to the point where she was really happy with all the work I was doing, and actually it had been quite a long time since she had been at all edgy.

I began to ride her around the farm and do a bit of work in the outdoor school too, and it all appeared to be going pretty well. Anyway,

17

The horse's mouth

after about a month I really did think I was onto something with the way I was doing things. What happened next I really regret – I should have been more careful. The only positive I can take from the situation is that from that day on I have taken even more care when it comes to looking after my horse.

A couple of my friends turned up with their horses and six or seven of us decided to ride out to the pub. I wanted to go a bit steady with my horse, so I opted to stay on the lanes rather than head out across the open moor. I had clearly said that I wanted a quiet ride in order to continue the good work I had been getting from my horse. Anyway, my two friends assured me they were happy to have a quiet ride too, and they opted to join me.

We hadn't gone far when I realised that my friends were riding what I would pretty much deem to be untrained animals. They had no effective brakes or steering – it was very much a 'point and hope' situation. For about 15 minutes I was feeling pretty chuffed: despite all the chaos, my horse was really calm and mentally like a rock. I actually remember I was thinking fairly smug thoughts along the lines of, 'Well, at least my horse is quiet,' as we rode down the lane between the trees. And then it happened. We were in single file with me in the middle, and the horse at the back was having some problems about not being next to its mate. Suddenly, horse and rider barged past us, knocking us sideways into the hedge. 'Sorry, coming through!' was the accompanying message as they charged along, completely out of control.

From that moment my horse seemed to forget everything I had been working on with her for the past few weeks and reverted to her old anxious self. We made it to the pub and I decided to ride off on my own to try to rebuild my horse. I managed to get quite a lot done on the way home, but for several days afterwards I was pretty down about what had happened. I was sad about my horse and I had lots of doubts about whether it was going to be possible to sort things out for her completely – in fact, and this might be linked to my age, this was also the point at which I seriously began to wonder about all the less anxious horses out there and whether they are the ones we should really be working with.

So, hopefully you now have a horse with a nice soft mouth and a good relationship with the bit. From here, if you are confident that you are safe to do this, you can stand in front of your horse, take the bit in your hands and walk backwards while encouraging your horse to come with you. Work towards leading him around the school in this way, following the bit with no leans and no pulls from him. And then, when you are confident that this is all going well, you can work towards doing a nice steady halt, in balance.

If you are struggling with the halt because your horse leans on the bit when you ask for it, gently raise his head and neck by lifting the bit a little, to rebalance him front to back just before you ask him to stop. This is a very important piece of information that I will discuss in a lot more detail later. For now, if you can get a balanced halt happening nicely, where the horse stops without propping himself up by putting weight on the bit, that in itself will begin to lead you towards working your horse in balance.

Now we are going to add in what a lot of people refer to as 'flexions'. I have actually heard a well-known horse trainer warn people off using Baucher's flexions, saying that you need years of training with a master before you can even attempt them. My reply to that would be, 'What utter rubbish!' Having said that, I will also note that Baucher's flexions changed a lot over the course of his life, and the way that I do the flexions is actually my way of doing them, as the way that you do them will be your way, if you see what I mean. Lots of people practise variations on these flexions and, if you are a reasonably sensitive horseman, as hard as I try I cannot see how you can cause damage to your horse by doing this. I can see how you could get it a bit wrong and teach your horse a few things that later you might wish he didn't know, but compared to most of what goes on with horses I reckon it's pretty safe territory. I think over the years there has been a slight feeling among some so-called classical riders that Baucher's flexions were and still are some kind of secret information. Well, if they are, the secret is well and truly out now. Plenty of western riders practise similar flexions and have done for years, and you can find them described in lots of books too.

Have your horse in a bridle. I prefer to use a bit with cheekpieces – remember what I said about the less movement in the mouth the better, as horses hate the feel of a bit that pulls sideways through the mouth. Stand in front of your horse and softly take the bit rings in each hand. Now ask the horse to release his jaw and give you a soft, mobile mouth.

If that is all working well with no resistances, gently lift the bit it into the right-hand corner of your horse's mouth to ask him to bend his head to the right. What you are looking for here is an obvious bend – 'flexion' – at the joint between the skull and the first neck vertebra (technically known as C1). You are not after a bend throughout the whole neck, and you don't want a big swing from the base of the neck. You need to isolate the response to this ask so that it is clear in the horse's mind – you are looking for a soft bend at C1 only. You also need to be sure that you don't accept a twist from upright in the horse's head, so that his nose tips up to one side (that would come from the joint between C1 and C2). Sometimes, if a horse is wary of giving at C1 he will use a twist as a way of protecting himself from doing so.

So let's run through this again point-by-point.

1. Stand at the front of the horse and hold the bit
2. Ask for a soft mouth
3. Raise the bit into the corner of the mouth and ask for a C1 bend
4. Move to the side and ask for more C1 bend
5. You do not want a bend through the whole neck
6. You do not want a bend at the base of the neck
7. You do not want the horse's head to tip from the vertical

Looking at the points 3 to 7 above, the only ones that actually get the result you want for your horse, the bend at C1, are numbers 3 and 4. For the horse to give you a good C1 flexion he genuinely has to release all the tension in his neck. The horse can easily carry out the other variations (points 5, 6 and 7) while still hanging on to his tensions and braces. And interestingly, those variations are all far more easily achieved than the one you want! Also take note that if you practise imperfect flexions you will be teaching your horse responses that later you will wish weren't in there. In other words, get it right from the beginning.

Once you have made a bit of a start on the right side you can move on to the left, or vice versa – you can do either side first, it doesn't matter.

So, why is this flexion important, and why is it important that you know why it is important?

When you ask your horse to bend at C1, you are effectively asking him to relax one side of his neck completely. To turn his head softly to the right at C1 he must allow all the muscles along the left side of his neck to relax and lengthen, and of course to turn his head to the left at C1 he must allow all the muscles on the right side of his neck to do the same. So, by using these flexions you can make a huge start on getting your horse to relax his whole neck.

In terms of training horses, relaxing the neck is quite a big deal. It is a physical and psychological release – I think this is because horses naturally use their necks for defensive purposes and are wary of letting go here. Some people call achieving relaxation of the neck a 'submission' by the horse, but to my mind the problem with that is it implies you are looking for some kind of domination. I would be trying to look at things from a more co-operative point of view. This might seem a small point, but to me it is pretty clear that the way you approach your horse work has a big effect on how the horse responds to you.

Later on we are going to talk about how the horse has to use

21

his body in order to carry a rider without putting undue strain on his physique. Part of this involves a relaxation of the back muscles along the horse's topline, so getting the mouth and neck to relax is a great place to make a start on this work.

And why is it important that you know why these flexions are important? Well, that comes down to the very heart of working with horses. You have to understand what you are doing and why you are doing it. If you don't have that knowledge, then you will surely come unstuck sooner rather than later. It is not enough to just blindly follow someone else's instructions, because for sure something will eventually happen where you need sufficient knowledge and confidence yourself to find a way of dealing with the situation.

If I think back a few years, what was my plan when I had difficulties with my horse? Well, I could ask someone for help, or if no-one was there I could try a few random ideas, or maybe I could lose my temper and try doing some crazy stuff. Or more recently when I first started working in public, if I got into a tricky situation I would often try to talk my way out of it. None of the above techniques are of much help to the horse. And that is the joy of Baucher's work: it is logical and easy to understand, for both the human and the horse. If right now you are maybe finding all of this a little bit vague, or if you are struggling to put into practice what I have described so far, I would strongly advise you to hang on in there, because I promise you that in the end it does all add up.

Once you have mastered the basic horsemanship skills that enable you to work your horse with no mental resistances from him, then you need to know how to train and work in a way that cares for him physically while he does the things you need him to do. And you don't have to be superman to understand how to do this – I am the living proof of that.

2 BRACES, RESISTANCES, SOFTNESS AND FEEL

I watched the trainer working with Sam for quite a while. He had already explained that there was a huge brace in the horse's neck, and he had been working for some time to take it out. I was watching, trying desperately to understand and learn what he was talking about. And then all of a sudden he would say, 'Ah yes, there we go, that feels better doesn't it, boy?' He started stroking the horse and took a break for a minute or two before carrying on. The next time everything happened much more quickly, and after a couple more little sessions the trainer pronounced, 'Now, there we are, let's see how that all feels in the morning.'

The whole thing was a mystery to me. It took me quite a long time to work out what was going on there but over the months I did, and oh boy did it change the way I looked at horsemanship. I began to get a picture of the kind of relationship I wanted with my horse.

So, what is a brace? Well, a brace is when you ask your horse to do something and he doesn't willingly do it. That's not strictly true of course, because maybe you'll be asking your horse to do something and he simply isn't hearing you. Or maybe he thinks he doesn't have to listen to you because you are simply not worth listening to. Or maybe you are asking him to do something that he simply physically can't do. So, for this question to be answered maybe we have to assume that you have a reasonably good working relationship with your horse. He understands that he needs to listen to you, and he also understands that when you ask him to do something he needs to make a bit of a try to do it.

Now, if you aren't at that situation with your horse, then in my view you need to get there. That's not necessarily going to take forever, but it is work that needs to be done. If you don't want to do that work, or maybe you want some other arrangement with

23

your horse, well, I'd say let's just leave it at that for now, and if you ever decide you want to change things around and go down this road, well, you can always give it a try then.

Up to now we have talked about two basic exercises – training the horse to relax his jaw for a soft, mobile mouth, and training him to bend at C1. Let's look at what to do if things don't work out with these two jobs.

I stand in front of my horse and softly take hold of the bit. My intention is to ask my horse to relax his jaw when I gently raise the bit into the corners of his mouth, towards his ears. But my plans are soon shot out of the water because my horse decides that my holding the bit like that is too much a problem for him to cope with. He starts to throw his head around, and occasionally dive his nose into the bit to try to find a way of changing the situation. So what am I going to do?

My first response is always to do as little as possible. That way, I don't add to the problems that the horse already has. At the same time, I am pretty determined that I want my horse to work things out and discover that the bit isn't a problem for him. So, as far as possible I try not to let him find any success in the head throwing or pushing, and at the same time show him that standing still and relaxing with the bit in his mouth is always an option.

I think I may need to explain this more clearly, so I'll give it a try. Because I have seen so many horses benefit hugely from having a clear understanding of the bit, I am pretty committed to getting this job done. Now, with a baby horse it's usually a formality and in no time at all they realise that the bit is a pretty nice means of communication. But sometimes with an older horse where there is a lot of history with the bit, things aren't always so straightforward.

The phone rang and the lady began to tell me all about her horse. I'd already heard a little bit about him on the grapevine and had expressed a slight interest in hearing more. The horse was called Ben. He was a

14-year-old, 16 hands Irish sports horse who had competed at eventing (show jumping, cross country and dressage) and he had hunted regularly. But for about the last year he had been intermittently lame and the owner had decided enough was enough. I asked her if the horse was still shod, which he was. At the time I was getting a bit fired up about barefoot riding being the answer to a lot of lameness, so I decided we should go and take a look at Ben, with the idea that taking his shoes off might make all the difference.

We arrived at Ben's home and met the owner, a very pleasant and knowledgeable lady called Jan. We went straight out to the paddock to meet Ben. Jan tacked him up and rode him around a bit to show us that he was ok. Then Sarah had a ride on him and it all looked pretty good. We only really needed him because he was a nice, strong horse and some of the kids in a project we were running at the time were pretty big. Then I got up on him – and it didn't take many seconds to feel how well trained he had been to lean on the bit. And I can tell you this: there was a lot to Ben, so that lean was pretty damn heavy.

I remember sitting up there, trying to get Ben to come back off the bit and balance up a little, with Jan saying, 'That's what he needs Tom, he needs to get that weight off his front feet.' Man was she right, he really did need to do that and maybe, just maybe, that would be enough to sort out his lameness.

These days I would just keep quiet at that point, but back then I had got a little bit beyond myself and I took the opportunity to give an explanation. 'Do you know that a horse in the field carries around 60% of his weight on his front feet and 40% on his back feet? And then, when you put a rider on him, he has 70% of the weight on the front and 30% on the back? That 10% could be what makes all the difference. If you balance him back up again, he could be fine.' That all sounds terribly trite to me now, but that's the way I was. We're making some progress there, which has got to be good!

Anyway, we set off home with Ben, me full of confidence and Sarah giving me the usual 'When will you ever learn?' speech. Jeez, how many more times do I have to listen to that one?

Braces, resistances, softness and feel

I'd done quite a bit of work with horses that had problems with the bit, but never ever had I come across one that leant the way Ben leant. His whole posture was sort of falling forward too – the tops of his front legs were about six inches ahead of the bottoms and I should think anyone could clearly see the bulk of his weight was on his front feet. I started off confidently, which I pretty much always do, but as time went on I realised that I was working with a very committed horse.

Over the years, Ben had learned that he could use the rider and the bit to help him carry the weight of his head and neck. That's fair enough too, because by no-one ever telling him otherwise he had been taught that it was OK. But for me it is useless. I am not prepared to carry that load when I am riding a horse – I'd rather get off and walk.

Ben was determined that he could lean on the bit and I was determined that he couldn't. It was a meeting of opposites – I could feel what you might call 'some resistance', and I guess he could too. All I was looking for was for Ben to carry the weight of his own head and neck, so every time he asked me to carry that weight for him – which to start with was 100% of the time – I asked him to stop doing that. And I asked him by standing in front of him holding the bit, and lifting it into the corners of his mouth to ask him to hold his head up himself. If he totally ignored me I changed from using a soft ask to a small vibration, where I lifted the bit about an inch and then relaxed and did it again in quick succession. This is not a violent move – it just avoids the possibility of the horse just leaning even more, because he simply can't lean on that kind of movement.

After about half an hour of Ben trying everything he knew to keep things as he had learned, including violently throwing his head and skewing his neck, there was suddenly a tiny change in him where I felt that at last he was beginning to look for an alternative solution. Throughout all of this I had done my utmost to provide a clear goal for Ben to find. I had added as little movement into what I was doing as I could manage. As a general rule it is crucial to do this – trying to teach the horse a lesson in a punitive way by exaggerating your responses to his movements is utterly counterproductive and futile. That is not what

26

this is about at all. We want to try to show the horse that the bit is reliable and constant, and something he can happily work with.

Once a horse gives you that tiny opening, it doesn't usually take long to move things along quite nicely. The resistances in Ben became less powerful and the tries became more willing, until after about three-quarters of an hour he was standing there, in balance, with the bit quietly sitting in his mouth. We'd made a start!

How does all this softness and feel work then, and what exactly do we mean by those words? I think the word 'feel' in relation to working with horses probably originated in the States, and I think that maybe the nearest equivalent in Europe is the classical term 'equestrian tact'. As far as I can see, it is absolutely essential that you get feel and softness happening in your horsemanship. Why do I say this? Because I'm pretty certain that you could understand all the theory in the world, and you could know every technique that every horseman has come up with for every situation you could ever end up in, but without feel it just isn't going to work. Your horsemanship simply isn't going to add up for the horse. So what are these elusive qualities?

Well, they are not just something physical, but that is a good place to start. Have your horse wearing a headcollar, then take hold of the lead rope and through it ask your horse to move his head towards you. See how small an ask you can use to get this to happen, and be sure to factor in all the responses that you get from your horse. Feel is a two-way communication between you and your horse – it is about the two of you working in harmony.

Now put your hand gently on your horse's chest and ask him to take one quiet step backwards. Can you both do this?

Now put your hand on your horse's flank and ask him to move sideways, just one step. Can you and your horse do this?

Now take hold of the cheekpiece of your horse's headcollar and ask him to bend his head gently towards you at C1. Can you both do this? Now try the other side. And now ask for the C1 bend and walk him in a small circle, keeping the bend. And now get a nice halt with no lurching or loss of balance.

Lots of things have to be in place between you and your horse for you to get all these jobs done nicely, and of course it may well be that you are both there already. You need your horse's attention, and you need his willingness to try to do whatever you ask him to do. You also need to be able to ask softly for things yourself, and to be able to read and factor in your horse's responses in each moment as you go along.

So, if you take the lead rope and gently ask your horse to turn his head towards you, and the first response you get is a pretty firm pull against you in the opposite direction – what are you going to do? The answer is totally logical. If you give to the horse and let him take the lead rope wherever he wants to, you have just succeeded in teaching him that your ask means nothing. If you resist the pull from the horse, and he then quits pulling and comes back to you, then you have just begun to teach him that your ask needs to be answered in that way.

What you can see in the above example is that behind your soft ask there needs to be absolute firmness. That is how and why softness works – because it is non-negotiable and it has no grey areas. I certainly wouldn't want to have too many rules around the place, but if I can have one rule it has to be that if you ask a horse for something you *have* to get it, or at the very least something roughly in the direction of what you are asking for.

Let's take a very different situation that uses exactly the same principles. Suppose you ask your horse to go from a halt to a walk and for this you use a nice soft leg cue. And then suppose that your horse walks off half asleep and with absolutely minimum effort. Now, if you accept that response on his part you are teaching him that that is precisely what you want. So what are you going to do? You have to find some firmness behind your soft ask, so in future he knows that when he feels your first soft ask he has to come through with exactly the goods you require. What that firmness is would be up to you. It could be all sorts of things. Just do what you have to do until what you have asked for comes through, and then release. You will have a soft, alert, willing horse in no time.

Some people really struggle with the idea of having unlimited firmness behind their first soft ask, and that is a problem. The biggest reason it's a problem is that your horse will know that, and consequently will factor that knowledge into everything that happens between you and him. If you think about it, the position a horse takes in the herd is completely dependent on how much firmness he has behind his softness. Ironically, if you are totally committed to having unlimited firmness behind your ask the horse will know that too, and this will allow you to get most, if not all, jobs done in a quiet, polite way.

If you do not incorporate feel and softness into your work, then what you will likely end up with is a light horse but not a soft one. A light horse feels at best slightly separate from you, in that your movements and responses aren't quite synched up. An example might be when you ask him to gently move sideways for one step: what you might get is sideways with no problem, but with no control over how many steps your horse takes. It is not a measured response to your ask; sometimes it even feels as if the horse is slightly running away from you.

Occasionally in the past I have heard the odd little gem of horse-trainer wisdom, and when I do there is always a small part of me that wants to hang on to it and not share it with anyone, but this one is good and I am happy to share it. I remember one day we were hanging around with Mark. We were having a bit of a laugh and Mark was there being his normal quiet self. Then he just said straight out of nowhere, 'Do you know how to make a light horse soft, Tom?'

I thought for a moment, and then answered, 'Good question Mark, I've never really thought about it before, and no I don't.'

'I'll tell ya how Tom. Get him to think,' was Mark's brief reply.

Braces, resistances, softness and feel

I've thought about that a lot since then. In fact, this little piece of knowledge plays a big part in the way that I am with horses. Only the other day we were working with a horse that was a wee bit sketchy and I said, 'What we need to do here is get this horse to think,' and that is just what we did. We gave him a few little jobs to do and after a minute or two he began to settle down and become engaged in the process, and then we started to get some good work done. It's not always so easy, but I'd say it's always true.

What thinking does to a horse is bring him right back into his body, right here in the moment. Some horses are so done in by everything people have done to them over the years that they have taken the decision that the safest place to be is anywhere but in their own body. It's their way of coping with the cards they have been dealt. Sometimes you will see a horse who mentally leaves the situation by wanting to be somewhere else so badly that they cannot focus at all on what is happening where they are physically, and other times you might see a horse that mentally leaves by just disappearing inside himself. The solution to both situations is to get the horse thinking. Try to show him that it is actually OK to be right here and happy with what is going on, then you can make a start on helping him to be a soft horse.

I just want to say a little more about horse's thinking. Horses don't use words in language, so how do they think? Well, I'm pretty sure they don't. Using the words 'thinking' and 'thought' in the above paragraphs is slightly incorrect, but I'm sticking with it because I think the idea of getting a horse to think, and of horses having thoughts, makes the job easier for humans to do. In fact, a better word might be 'focus', and actually what brings the horse back into the situation is that he feels that it is more comfortable to be there than it is to be away. What he doesn't do is logically work anything out – he follows his feelings. This is fairly crucial information relating to the art of horse training because when you understand that what motivates horses is their need to feel good, then if you can provide that feeling, you are in business.

30

Braces, resistances, softness and feel

ᡣ

Let's get back to working closely with our horse, and look at how we would deal with a brace in his neck if we ask him via the cheekpiece of the headcollar to bend softly at C1. Maybe what we get is nothing at all in terms of bend; what we do get is a pretty stiff neck that really doesn't want us messing about like this, and there is quite a bit of pushing and nose poking, and then we start thinking, 'Oh my, why did I get involved in this, and damn, now I have to find some way out of here, oh my, oh my, I could just quit.' But the problem is that we have asked, and we don't want to break the 'rules' so we realise we are committed to at least getting something, however small, somewhere in the direction of what we want.

So we hang on in there, holding onto the headcollar, and through all the chaos we keep our ask there for the bend, and pretty much always there comes a point where the horse seems to think, 'This isn't going away, I have to look for a solution to it.' And that is when you feel the first little try. And there, right at that point, your horse feels his first little release, right there in your soft hold on the headcollar. Right there, right at the moment of his first try, you went from being quite firm to being very soft, and your horse, because he is a horse, felt what you just did as easy as anything, and that's it – you've made a good start on that job.

So, that's braces, resistances, softness and feel sorted out. Now that we all understand these basics of horsemanship, we can crack on and get some work done.

3 MORE ABOUT THE BIT

The next job is to take the results we got organised in chapter 1 and start to transfer them from the bit rings to the reins. First we'll do this from the ground, and when that is all working well we'll try it from on top.

Stand on the left side of your horse next to his head and take the right-hand rein over the top of his neck, so that you can hold it with your right hand. Hold the left-hand rein with your left hand, just where it connects to the bit. Now you can simulate exactly what you were doing from in front of the horse, but this time you are using the reins. Practise getting a soft mouth and then have a go at the flexions.

If you are standing on the left side of your horse, it's generally a good idea to go for the right-hand flexion first, as most horses find this set-up easier to understand. Stand your horse up square and, holding the reins as described above, lift his head and neck so that the poll is the highest point and there is no weight on the bit. Then put a feel on the right rein to lift the right-hand side of the bit into the corner of your horse's mouth. At the same time use your left hand to hold a neutral contact in the left-hand side of the bit and gently push your horse's head around to bend at C1. Most horses grasp this without too much trouble, especially if you have got them really good at it already by working from in front.

At first when you do this, you might well feel as if there is so much going on that you can't really cope very well. It is surprising how quickly you get the hang of it all though, but I do admit I do often miss out some of the details by mistake. It goes without saying (so why I am saying it?) that it is obviously better to do it all correctly. One thing it is good to remember though, is that you should ask for a soft mouth before and after each flexion. If you do this you pretty much know that you have a relaxed and happy horse at the beginning and end of each section of the job. For a horse to give you a soft mouth he must be relaxed himself, and also he must be in balance. If you yourself try walking along a narrow beam you will see that any tension you hold is a massive handicap to balancing. This also works in reverse. If you go out of balance you tense up. This is something to think about for later – tenseness leads to loss of balance, and loss of balance leads to tenseness. One of the most well known sayings attributed to Baucher is '*Balance before movement*' – I'd actually say it is almost a golden rule.

Once you have the right flexion working nicely move around to the other side and get the left one working, by doing everything the same way but in reverse. And then see if you can get both flexions working from each side by bringing the head towards you too. All of this should be happening in a pretty relaxed and flowing sort of way. You can tell a huge amount about the horse's state of mind by how he feels when you do the flexions. He might feel twitchy, like he doesn't really want to be there, or you might feel resistances which you need to help him through. Whatever it all feels like and however easy or difficult it is, over a few days you should expect it to come pretty good. If you're having to use anything more than a soft touch to get this job done then you still have a bit more work to do.

I want to try and describe the feeling that you need to have in your hands, and in the whole of you really too. It is a soft feeling but it's not a tentative feeling. It is re-assuring and definite, but not threatening. If the horse resists there is firmness there, but not something that will bring fear to the horse. If the horse meets firmness and gives to it, then softness is right there for him. If the horse meets firmness and pushes into it he meets more firmness, but again not something that will frighten him. I would say also, that that firmness never moves towards the horse – it is something that the horse can ease off from and right there he finds softness.

I can see how someone might not understand how you can ask the horse to move his head say, and if the horse then resists, how can you get firm and not move your ask towards the horse. This is almost a mystery isn't it, but it's not – softness only works if there is firmness behind it. It is being able to get firm but in that firmness there is no push (or pull). There is a soft ask and right behind it is firmness that doesn't give way but also doesn't push. If the horse gives to the ask he instantly feels the release – it's there in the ask – the horse can feel it most times before he even thinks about resisting it. That's why some people look good working with horses – because they know that feeling and they can get that to work for them.

A really good way to feel this softness is to work with a baby horse. Get a headcollar and lead rope on them and hold the rope and wait for the foal to check it out. He will take up the slack in the rope up to until he starts to feel it, and if you just stay put with a nice soft feel on the rope, he will check it out and come back off the pressure. The pressure he is coming off is the pressure that he put on himself. He is working things out for himself there, and all you are doing is holding the rope. If you try to make things any more complicated than that you are just not helping that foal at all. And that's how it is with horses too. Try to keep it that simple.

And so what do you do if you end up working with a horse that doesn't keep things that simple? Say you ask him to do something and he just can't handle it. Well, the first thing is to try and judge that the horse is going to be ok with your ask, and mostly you'll get that right but sometimes you'll get it wrong – that's horsemanship, and we all get things wrong now and again. So if I misjudge what I ask of my horse and he lets me know it, I go back and try again with an ask that I think he will be ok with. This is hard to discuss really, because it comes down to all sorts of personal stuff I guess. I'm hesitant to say 'push things on' because that way you take more risks, but I'm really hesitant to say 'take your time' because that way you can soon teach your horse that you have all day and he doesn't really need to bother too much. You have to find the middle path, or at least the path that suits you – I'm not sure anyone can help anyone else sort that one out.

❀

And so back to the flexions. We have a joke in our yard that your horse's C1 joint should be like a well-oiled hinge. I don't think it is far from the truth really. Ideally, I like to feel my horse follow the bit wherever it goes. When I bend his head to one side I want him to just stay there until I ask him to bend back to straight. Remember if your horse has a relaxed mouth and neck you are well on the way to having a relaxed horse.

❀

Before we go any further with this there is one very important thing that you need to know and fully accept about your hands and the bit. This is pretty much an unbreakable rule too, I'd say. When your horse is going forwards the bit must never go backwards in other words if you imagine that your arms hang down straight from your shoulders, and that your elbows line up perfectly with your body, then there should never be a time when your elbows go backwards.

And here is an exercise for you to try which will make you understand why this rule is a must to stick with. Have a friend stand about a metre behind you and take some reins around your waist. You hold on the reins with both hands in front of your belly button and have your friend hold on to the reins so he/she can guide your direction. Start off by walking together and asking your friend to direct you. He must use as little ask as possible to get the message through to you. Can you feel any backwards pull, and if so what do you think? Now ask him, instead of pulling back, could he please just try asking with the same amount of feel but by taking the rein to the side and really trying hard not to put any backward pull on it. Is that more comfortable?

Now ask him to take a more firm contact and generally be more workmanlike about the whole thing. If your friend is a horseman ask him to simulate how most people use the reins. What do you think of that? And that's what most horses have to put up with, and on top of that, it's all happening in their mouth.

35

More about the bit

So what does this mean in practical terms? It means that when you want to turn your horse you cannot use the reins to mechanically pull him around the corner. You have to start by having a cue that the horse clearly understands means to turn. Later, when things are a bit more progressed, the horse will turn when you turn.

Doing the flexions from the ground you should notice that the angle of the reins roughly simulates the angle that you will use to do the flexions when you are riding your horse too. You should be gently lifting the bit up towards the ears and into the corners of the mouth. By lifting the bit in this way you never run the risk of hurting the horse by putting pressure on the tongue. This is very important – the tongue needs to be free. Psychologically and physically this is absolutely crucial. The horse must feel free and there is no way that is going to happen if he has his tongue pinned down. And physically, in order to balance all his muscles must be relaxed and free from tension. The horse's tongue must be relaxed – it is not a co-incidence that our very first job was to ask for a relaxed mouth.

Just as an experiment, next time you get tense take notice of where the tension is manifesting physically in your body. I'm pretty certain one of the first areas you will tense up will be your jaw and tongue – yep, nice and tight, eh, I thought so!

Now we are going to get the flexions working nicely while we are walking along. Again I'm happy to have the help of a friend here. Sometimes the horse can't believe you are asking them to move as well as flex so I think making the training process as simple as possible is a good idea.

Stand at the side of your horse and take the reins as described above, only this time you can have your hand that holds the outside rein further back on your horse's mane. This actually simulates even more the position of the rein while you are riding. Now ask the horse to move forward in a walk. If you have a voice cue here, or a click or kiss that works for walk that can help, or if you are pretty

36

deft with a schooling whip you can use that. The down side of the whip idea is that moving your hand also moves the bit, which I think is pretty unhelpful. What I do, if I get stuck, is get another person to encourage the horse to move from behind. The horse pretty soon works out what the job is. At this point I am not asking for bend – I am looking to establish a forward cue that works really well so that when we do ask for the flexions we don't just grind to a halt, or if we do, we at least have some hope of moving forward from there.

Get the walk working really well in both directions, with you on either side, and make sure that the whole thing is happening without any weight or pressure between you and the horse. The next thing to try is to see if you can change the height of your horse's head and neck before you set off, and also while you are walking along. The ability to be able to do this is crucial because this is how we can begin to have some say in the balance of the horse. Remember in chapter one where I was describing coming into the halt in balance – if the horse isn't balanced as he comes into the halt, he will fall forward onto the bit. So the way that we can help him in that situation is by raising his head and neck. This isn't necessarily a huge thing, it can be tiny, but the fact is for it to happen the horse has to be open to the idea, and also he has to be free from bracing against it.

To be honest, once you've had a bit of practice at this work it's all pretty easy with most horses. If you have good feel (or are developing good feel) and you have created (or happen to have) a nice soft horse, you can really rattle through this part of the work. For example, if your horse knows to move away from you, then one thing you can try is to set off walking in a circle and then try and enlarge the circle. You should be able to feel the horse stepping away from you and moving his shoulders out on to the bigger circle. Then you could try making the circle smaller – this time you should feel the horse moving his shoulders towards you on to the smaller circle. Don't worry if this doesn't work out too well – all this kind of thing will get sorted out as we add in moving the shoulders later on. Remember, the further that you go with this work, the more flexible and gymnastic your horse will become.

ᧉ

Maybe now is a good time to talk some more about the relationship between the horse's mouth and the bit. Hopefully if you have been practising these exercises you will already be getting a glimpse of a different relationship between the mouth and the bit to that which most horses have to get used too.

Let's look at some of the things that horse's get asked to do in relation to the bit. At this point I am not going to look at the riders and trainers who don't really know what deal they want in this area – maybe we can go into that later. Here we're going to study a couple of training methods where the use of the bit is clearly understood. I'll just say here, it's not that many years ago that I had no idea what was supposed to be going on at the end of my reins, but then I had a bit of a breakthrough. I worked out that if I presented the bit to my horse in a consistent way, then my horse had a better chance of coming up with a consistent response himself.

At the time I was pretty impressed by what might loosely be called, 'the western scene'. I liked the idea of having a light feel in my hands and a horse who would listen to the smallest ask from the bit. I also really liked the way, when you picked up the reins the horse would kind of come alive and get ready to go. The whole quarter horse thing of going to sleep when nothing is happening, but being 100% ready to work when needed, really appealed to me too. So I began to build this into my horse. I taught my horse to never ever lean on the bit, in fact, if you think about how she related to the bit, she knew that the comfortable place for her to have the bit was to have it sitting just lightly resting on her lower jaw. When we were going forwards there would be no weight in my hands and the bit would be right there, resting on her lower jaw. If I moved the bit backwards she was always right there moving backwards just ahead of it. I had her travelling just behind the bit.

38

It actually felt great to me and there is no denying we got a lot done like that. I rode her around on a pretty slack rein and I never ever felt any weight in my hands. I had fingertip control, we could back up like a dream, and we had pretty good brakes too. So that's one way of riding and from my point of view at that time, it worked pretty well.

Another way of riding involves training your horse to accept weight on the bit. Now, here I have to say I am not an expert on this system (not that I am on the other system either) so I may get some of the terminology and aims wrong, so please forgive me for that. But I am sure most people have heard somewhere along the line that the weight that they should feel in each hand through the reins, is the equivalent to a bag of sugar. In reality this weight between the human and the horse happens at the point of contact, which is the bit. Of course the required contact is going to vary from person to person and horse to horse, but the principle is the same – have a constant contact of some weight and through that contact, communicate your needs.

In the first system, imagine the bit in the horse's mouth. The job of the horse is to get just behind it. When you pick up the reins and put a slight upward feel into the bit, the horse comes up just above the feel. If you move the bit backwards the horse, depending on how he has been taught, will either curl his neck down behind the bit, or actually back up to stay just behind the bit.

In the second system the horse is effectively, physically pushing into the bit. It's the exact opposite to the first system. To move the horse's head you have to manually move the bit against the horse's pressure. If you want to back up I'm not sure how you do that – I'll just go and ask Sarah, hang on a sec. Ha ha ha, not sure if I should write this or not, but here we go. 'You put your legs quite far back and then kind of rhythmically pull back quite hard, a bit like rowing a boat. It's not pretty,' she said.

Anyway, I'm sure there are plenty of people out there who can back up perfectly well with pressure in their hands – and that's not

39

at all related to the point I'm trying to make at the moment. What I want to try and explain is that what Baucher worked out and designed, was a system of communication between the horse and rider where the horse's mouth and the bit were connected, as one harmonious unit. The bit and the mouth move together in a totally harmonious way. The mouth is not moving away from the bit, as in the first system, and it is not leaning into the bit as in the second system. There is no pressure and no force – but there is a soft, happy, and mobile mouth that fully accepts the bit, and is connected to a soft, happy, and mobile horse.

This is what I am endeavouring to explain in this book. And the reason I am trying to do this is because since I came across Baucher's work, I, as a very average and fairly unadventurous horseman, have had so much fun riding my horse. I have no great ambition – I check my cows, I occasionally ride out with Kate, and I mess about in the school doing bits and pieces. I like moving around sideways and stuff like that, but I couldn't care less about anything fancy, and in saying that I am not in any way belittling or disparaging that kind of work. I fully understand that if you want to improve the health, well being and longevity of your horse, then studying and practising dressage (in the correct sense of the word) is not only an extremely effective thing to do, it is the correct thing to do, and it is also thoroughly enjoyable.

Finally, it's time to get on your horse and try asking for a soft mouth. Try to replicate the cue that you were using from the ground. It's not always easy by the way. If you are finding it really difficult to start with, one thing I have tried is to have a friend on the ground to help. That way your friend can step in and help by using the short reins if you get stuck. And then you can gradually pass the cue over from the short reins to the long reins.

If the mouth is working nicely then try asking the horse to carry his head a little higher. Get the poll of the horse as his highest point and have a go at the flexions. Get both sides working nicely

– remember the well-oiled hinge. If all that is in place try walking around a bit and asking for the flexions as you turn – if you can get this happening nicely you are really on the way to having a pleasant riding horse.

Let's look at what needs to be in place for all this to happen. Your horse needs to have a relaxed mouth and a relaxed neck. He needs to be pretty focussed, or perhaps we could put it another way, he mustn't be too distracted. He needs to be listening to you and ready to do what you ask. In return you must offer your horse simple instructions that he understands, and that are not going to blow up in his face for reasons he doesn't understand. You need to have softness in your state of mind and in your body. This all sounds pretty nice doesn't it – no wonder horses like it.

4 BALANCE

A few years ago Sarah and I used to travel around the country a bit doing horse-training clinics. We really enjoyed it and most of the time it was good fun, but at the same time it was quite often very challenging. Some nights we would end up in our room chatting into the early hours about all the jobs we were involved in with all the different riders. The truth is, we were obsessed and we loved it.

Looking back I can see that one of the main problems we had was that we didn't have a complete paradigm of how to train a horse. There were areas of training that we were not clear about and we were definitely working things out a bit as we went along. If you are reading this now and you were a client of ours at that time, please don't pick up the phone and ask for your money back. Well, you can if you like but I'll tell you to go away because in general, as far as I can see, that's what most horse trainers are doing anyway.

We knew we didn't have a system, and anyway, we knew that the majority of people we worked with were already involved in systems that they had picked up from other trainers. Occasionally we would end up working with the odd person who had somehow managed to stay system-free, and generally this was because they were either new to working with horses, or they had recently become totally disenchanted with the way they were being taught and we were the first trainers they had come across since they reached that conclusion. Actually we often heard it said that because we didn't have a system some people found it quite a struggle to work with us.

The thing is that at that time we would work with anyone and any system because whatever anyone does there is always room for improvement. There are some things that are common to all good horsemanship and so we would work on those things. I used to have this little unplanned talk that I opened the clinics with, explaining that we were all here to work on and improve our horsemanship over the next few days etc, etc. The thing is that when it came to the horses my strength, if I had one, is that I did have some understanding of feel and softness, and the reason that I was able to stand up there and run clinics in the way that I did was that feel and softness can help everyone. Over the years I worked with people who said they were practising natural horsemanship right through to people who were doing quite intense competitive work, and generally I like to think I was of some help to most of them.

We always began each session by asking what the person would like to work on with us at the clinic. And then we'd say 'ok' and totally ignore what they had said and carry on doing whatever work we felt they needed to do. That is a joke by the way – of course we didn't do that. But sometimes it was hard to help people do what they wanted to do, simply because so much other stuff needed to be in place before it would be possible.

Towards the end of our clinic phase, this issue was becoming more and more apparent to us. We began to realise from the work we were doing with our own horses that if you built things up in some kind of order everything became a whole lot easier. And as hard as it was for me to admit it, horror of horrors I could see that even me, Tom Widdicombe, the fanatical anarchist horse trainer, was beginning to systemise my horsemanship.

It really came to a head at one of the last clinics we did when one girl asked us to help her to get her horse to canter. I clearly remember watching this girl trotting around on her horse, and me thinking there's no way that horse is going to go into a canter from there. I could see that the horse needed more balance so I went over to Sarah and talked to her about what I was seeing. 'Yep' she said, 'you're right, and yes, it does need more balance.' Now, that's not to say that horses can't canter without being balanced up front to back, they obviously can because most of them do. But here's how I see it – quite a few horses don't want to go into canter because they really don't like the feeling of losing their balance in that way. It becomes a self fulfilling prophesy for the horse really –

43

he doesn't want to canter because he doesn't like losing his balance, but he can't trot any faster so he has to go into canter, and yes, he was right, it feels awful because he has lost his balance, so then the next time he doesn't want to go into canter. So if we know how to avoid that situation in the first place why on earth would we not. I guess I've seen one too many horses being pushed into canter through a fast trot, when the truth is if you get everything set up correctly the same job can happen with virtually no worry about upsetting the horse.

And that was the beginning of the end of the clinic phase for me. I realised that this horse training malarkey was a total deal and cherry picking bits and pieces when it suited me was not something I could do any more.

I actually finally worked this out as I stood there in front of the girl and all of the audience too. I was all miked up so everyone got to listen as I explained my revelation. I talked them all through what I was thinking, and I could see a few people there were nodding in agreement. I explained that to train a horse correctly things needed to be put in place in a certain order, and each part of the training needed to be complete and correct before you moved on to the next part. If it wasn't in place correctly and you moved on, then that poor training would inevitably show up down the line, and not only that, all the subsequent jobs would be much more difficult than they should be. Horse training done correctly should be easy for you and the horse. If you come to a difficulty it's usually because something is not in place that should be, prior to the work that you are now doing.

I often wonder how many people listening to horse trainers actually realise that a lot of the time the trainers are learning the stuff right there in front of them. Not always of course – some know a lot and have seen a lot, and have a total paradigm that covers every situation that they come across. For the past few years I feel as if I have had a pretty consistent view of the job that I think needs to be done, but the nice thing is that at the same time as that I feel that I still have so much to learn. Every time I work with a horse I seem to come away thinking, 'mmm, I never quite realised that before'. And what I realise pretty much every time actually, is that the job is more simple than I thought it was. It's simple but it's difficult.

✑

As you read on please try and remember, I am not from a horsey background and although I had often heard people using expressions such as on the forehand, front-end-heavy, even-loading, and half halt, no-one had ever managed to explain to me exactly what they meant by them. But now suddenly, I felt as if I was beginning to get a glimpse of some things happening roughly around that area. Remember also, that by now I had started to explore with my own horses, what Baucher had been up to all those years ago. And, if I am honest, I was beginning to be fairly convinced of his wisdom.

I had been working with Splash, firstly with the flexions and then with experiments in balance. As I have already said, I had trained Splash to travel behind the bit. I found this preferable to her putting weight into the bit. But now I was changing things around. Now I wanted her to accept the bit and travel with it, rather than move away from it. I picked up the reins and asked her to change her balance from front to back until I could actually feel the point when the weight change between her front and back feet occurred. I was in effect rocking her weight back off her front feet and on to her hind feet. I then began to ask her to walk forward in this state of balance. At first I think she thought I was barmy, but as time went by I think she began to like the feel of it. We got quite good at it and I began to realise that actually it wasn't just Splash that was balancing; it was me too. We did in fact become one unit in balance.

From there I quickly took it further, and I found that because of her balance, moving her around was really good fun. A whole new world was opening up to me as I realised that our balance was the key to all kinds of useful stuff. Not only that; it was also the key to her peace of mind – she loved it. I don't know if this is true or not, but I have often said that the reason horses love balance is because they need to feel free to run – their DNA is telling them that at any time they may have to leave, and leave very fast too. Split seconds count for a lot in the life of the prey animal.

I began to see that once you show a horse that you know about balance, it feels a bit like the horse kind of goes, 'Phew, that's good, so you know about this too.'

❧

Tilly had taken about a year to start looking good after we had finally got around to weaning her foal. We've got far too many horses and we need to sell some. And Tilly came to the top of the list to try and get working and to see if we could sell her. We got her in a few times and she was actually quite a joy to work with. We didn't exactly know her breeding but she had come from France and had been described to us as an unregistered Andalusian. Now, if you've ever worked with Iberian horses you probably know that generally speaking they are usually pretty nice to work with. As with many breeds bred for serious work it sometimes feels as if it is almost in their genetic make up to look for and enjoy their work. Tilly felt like that.

The only thing we had difficulty with was that she really was not happy with the bit in her mouth. I tried her with the bit a few times and things didn't improve so I decided we should continue just working her on the headcollar. I put the saddle on and got Kate to practise as if she was going to get on, and I got her to gently bang around a bit to see how she coped with things going not so smoothly. Everything seemed fine so I asked Kate if she wanted to get on and she was ok with the idea.

We took Tilly to the mounting block and Kate quietly got on. Tilly was ok with that so I led her around a bit making sure I put in fairly sharp turns each way, and backed her up a few steps, and then I asked Kate if she felt ok about going free. She had no problems with that idea either so I quietly unclipped the lead rope and stood back a bit. What happened next really surprised me.

Kate asked Tilly to go forward and off she went as happy as anything. I noticed that Kate was balancing her up really well and I could clearly see that Tilly felt really secure in her work. They were putting in some pretty turns and then they did a perfect halt with no falling forward or loss of balance at all. Then they did a perfect back-up, halt, and set off forward again. It was all very pretty to watch.

Now, I don't want to jump to conclusions here, but I'm going to anyway. That was the first time I had ever seen a first ride done so well, and I couldn't help thinking that as soon as Tilly realised that Kate knew about balance, she felt good. Of course there is a very remote outside chance that Tilly had been ridden before in this way and she expected nothing less, but what are the chances of that – pretty low I'd say.

One day when the dentist was around I asked him to take a look in Tilly's mouth. Not only did he find one tooth had grown unbelievably long – I've never seen anything like it actually, it was about half an inch longer than all her other teeth – but she also had a small 'wolf' tooth hidden in her gum just where the bit would sit. The dentist sorted that all out and a few of days later we tried the bit again. Wow, she was like a different horse, so after a few minutes when it was completely clear she was ok, I started work on getting her mouth soft and introduced her to the flexions. Oh my, what a sweet little horse she is.

A couple of years ago we decided that we would no longer take in other people's horses to work on. We'd been doing it for years and it was hard work, and because we are so crap at business it was not always very profitable – we often ended up working for nothing because we felt bad about charging for the huge amounts of time we often put in. But the real reason we quit was because we had reached the conclusion that it was not a good idea for us to train a horse one way, and get him used to that, and then hand him back to someone who did things a completely different way. And then of course there was also the fact that we were having more fun just working with our own horses anyway.

But then the telephone rang and it was Joy. We'd worked for Joy before, many times. In fact we'd worked with the horse she was phoning up about. Magic was now four years old and he had been away to another trainer to be started. He was now home and Joy's rider was taking him

*out and about around the place. There were a few snags and could we
sort them out for her.*

*I asked Kate if she wanted the job of riding this horse on for a bit, and
she agreed to do it. We had a long conversation with Joy about how we
were training horses right now. We explained about the soft mouth and
the relaxed neck and so on, and perhaps more crucially, we explained
that once we had set up the horse in this way he would need to be
ridden on in the same way. Joy was happy with what we had told her and
actually she came over with a friend and spectated at a clinic for a day
as well. And at the end of the clinic day she still wanted Magic to come
over. Joy also volunteered that her rider would come over and work with
us too, to give Magic the best possible chance of success in the future.*

*There is so much to write about the job that we did with Magic, and I'll
do that later, but for now I'm going to tell you one thing. When he arrived
he wasn't what you might call a 'totally out of order' horse. He was ok
really, in relative terms, but not really quite how we would want our
horses to be around the place. The most interesting thing was the way
that he kind of crept forward all the time when you had him standing
on a lead rope. He didn't lead quite like we'd like him to either. He had
lost sight of the rules about boundaries and personal space that we had
shown him when he stayed here with us as a yearling. To put it politely,
he was all over you really.*

*So we were all standing in the barn with him and chatting, how you
do, and quietly asking him to stand still on the end of the rope, and he
kept creeping forward, and even when he did stand still you could kind
of feel him almost falling forwards. It was a strange feeling. And then we
saw that he was actually leaning forwards as he stood. It looked as if
his weight was pushing him forwards, and it also looked as if from that
stance, he couldn't really do anything else except move forwards.*

*Well, it was Kate's job so we let her get on with it. A couple of times
she mentioned that she was having to be pretty forthright about him
not pushing past her when she was leading him, but after a few days
she said it was starting to come quite nice. The next weekend Joy came
over to see how things were going and before she arrived I went down*

the barn to have a look at Magic. I thought, 'That's funny, he looks a bit different to me.' But I didn't say anything. And then when Joy arrived she said, 'Oh my, what have you done, doesn't he look beautiful.' Magic was standing there all proud, and the lean forward had totally gone. The truth is he was happily standing still, in balance, and feeling so much better for it.

The thing is if there is a forward push in your horse then you are on a loser before you even start. Everything about that forward push conspires against you getting any good work done. As far as I can see it does, anyway. Physically, he is a mess, and mentally he is a disaster. And yet how simple is it to make that small change that allows your horse to feel ok.

So there we have a couple of stories about a couple of different horses and how balance affected each of them. If you are in the situation that I was in, not being able to grasp or picture the concept of balance, I hope this has helped you.

Now let's try an exercise with a horse which should help make things even more clear. To do this exercise it's probably going to help if you use a horse that is already pretty familiar with the bit work described in the book so far. Stand in front of your horse and gently take hold of the bit. Ask the horse to give you a nice soft mobile mouth. Now, gently lift the bit up towards his ears with the idea that you are going to ask the horse to back up by changing his balance, rather than by pushing him backwards. As soon as you feel his body rock back, just before his feet move, just hold things there. Try that a few times so that you and the horse are ok with the idea. Now this time, get to that point and ask him to slowly walk forward in that balance.

You may feel lots of different things at this point. He may not be able to do it – you may feel him lean into the bit as he sets off – you may find he rushes forward and almost pushes through you – you may feel him lean into one side of the bit and try and push through his shoulder – you may feel his back end sort of try and squirm its way around you – or hopefully you may feel him take just

Balance

a few steps in perfect balance and come to a halt when you ask him to, without leaning on the bit at all.

I'd be pretty keen to get that last result.

It might take him a few seconds to work out what you are after

I know quite a few people will freak when they read about lifting the horse's head. I know for some people that it is almost a cardinal sin. I don't have a problem with it at all and very soon I will be explaining why not. I'd also like to say that if you are at all worried about anything in this book that I suggest you might do with your horse, then it has to be best that you don't do it. If you are in that situation then I'd suggest that you read the book to the end and see if it answers your doubts. If not and you still want to look further into this way of working, as I have already said in chapter one, spend time working alongside people who you trust and who are working in this way. Of course, if it's simply not for you, that's fine too – just leave it.

⥿

5 HOW TO SIT ON THE HORSE

You know, the idea of a human riding a horse is that when the person gets to their destination, the horse is tired because he has been working, but the human is fresh because he hasn't. So if you ever hear anyone say they are knackered after riding their horse, unless they have been absolutely miles and miles, you know they have been doing something wrong.

If you take the above statement as your guideline for riding then you will be half way there with regards to how to ride – you need to relax. The other half of the deal that you need to know is for the sake of the horse – you need to sit in balance. And don't say, 'Of course you do or you will fall off', because balance when you are sitting on a horse involves just a bit more than not falling off.

Occasionally people ask me if I can teach them to ride. These days I mostly say 'No'. Ironically, in the past, when I rode but didn't know how to, I used to say 'Yes', and I'd get paid for it too. That just about says it all about the deal the horse gets for getting mixed up with humans doesn't it.

Let's look at the two main things that I reckon you need to ride a horse: relaxation and balance. They are pretty closely linked because without relaxation you're not going to get balance. And here's the really interesting thing – the point when I started to understand balance was also the point when I really began to find relaxion. For years I have worked hard to relax on the back of a horse. I would check for tensions throughout my body, relax my legs, relax my arms, relax my back and so on and so on. Funnily enough the part I struggled with most, and maybe I should keep this to myself, was my backside. I couldn't seem to just sit softly in the saddle – my butt kept tensing up. I'm pleased to say that is all a thing of the past nowadays, but I don't want to get complacent. I am well aware that nothing lasts forever.

How to sit on the horse

So I would recommend that you work on both these qualities at the same time, because I am pretty certain they are closely linked. Get on your horse and relax. By relax I obviously don't mean slump, and that's where the balance comes in. Ask your horse to come back off the front end and balance and at the same time you get in balance with him, and then you both hold that position. Now take a look at how you are sitting. It will probably be pretty near perfect according to all the books that people write on this subject.

Here are some of the things that you can't be doing if you are sitting on your horse in balance. You won't have any tension in any of your muscles. You won't be involved in trying to maintain some kind of prescribed position. You won't be involved in maintaining muscle tone. You won't have a hollow back. You won't be slumping. And one thing you will be doing is sitting up pretty straight, but, and this is important, you won't be sitting there looking like you have a poker up your jacksy, you will be sitting there feeling pretty mobile and free. And all of this will be happening without you doing anything except relaxing and balancing.

If you are still reading this book, which of course I hope you are, please be patient. Reading back over the past few paragraphs I can see that some people are going to find some of that pretty abstract. And abstract is exactly what I promised myself this book wouldn't be. I want to try and use an analogy to explain how I feel about Baucher and his work, and my attempts at incorporating some of his ideas into my horsemanship.

Are you familiar with what might be loosely termed 'oriental philosophy'? I'm not going to get too carried away by it – this is a book about horsemanship, not how to live your life – but I am interested in the differences between the oriental and western ideas of how a person can find satisfaction. I'll lay my cards on the table right from the start. I am 100% a devotee of the oriental school (but I promise I will try and be as objective as possible).

In oriental philosophy the basic idea is that what you see outside of yourself is a reflection of what you are feeling inside of yourself. In other words if you want to live a peaceful and satisfying life you need to find peace and satisfaction within yourself. In contrast to that approach, in western society we are sold the idea that through the accumulation of wealth, fame and material goods (external stuff) we will have a rewarding and fulfilling life. Clearly these ideas are opposing. Needless to say some folks try living a sort of merged version of both ideas – as far as I can see that's called a mess, but not quite as much of a mess as it is when you exclusively chase wealth. My experience is that if I am on the ball, and I concentrate my energy into my inner experience, then what's out there tends towards taking care of itself.

I know this is a subject that when it is taken to the extremes, as described above, is quite controversial and some people may even find it confronting. But I am sure everyone will agree that if you wake up feeling good, then you are more tolerant of things going wrong than if you wake up feeling bad. That is a simple example of the truth behind oriental philosophy. So what has all this got to do with horses? Well, I see Baucher's work as very much about putting one thing in place so that everything else works. As opposed to the alternative approach which is to assemble all the different parts of the operation and getting things working that way. For example, if you see a rider on a horse and he is doing a really good job – maybe he is moving a bunch of cows through a tiny gap in a fence – then you could take a photo of him on his horse and then go away and look at how he is sitting and look at how his horse is travelling, and you could try and put all that in place yourself. It may be that the horse has a nice rounded neck, so you could use some straps to hold his neck in place. And maybe the cowboy's ankles are at a right angle, so you could work hard on that yourself. Maybe he is sitting pretty upright, so you could try and do that too. Maybe the horse's responses are pretty quick, so you could get some spurs, just like the cowboy's too, and so on and so on.

How to sit on the horse

Or perhaps, and this is the crucial point here, you could find one thing that you could do that would enable you and your horse to do all the separate things that the cowboy was doing. That thing is balance. Now, if you have that one thing it is actually quite likely that you will have most of the separate things too, but not necessarily. For example you can get balance with your ankles at any angle, and what about those old boys who ride their horses till they die – they know about balance and they can't sit up straight. What about riders who have physical disabilities – I know at least two – one girl I know, her whole left side is knackered from a stroke and she's a really pretty rider.

Let's briefly talk about breathing. It is closely and utterly linked to relaxation. Some people do link their breathing in quite a big way to the actions they do in their riding. I have never got involved in this myself so I'm not going to say much about that side of things. But what I have practised over the years is being aware of my breath. Again, I don't know if I need to say this, but horses are very sensitive creatures and I am pretty certain that the state of your breathing is registered by them whenever you are around them. I think it is worth thinking about. Of course it's difficult to manufacture relaxation – again I'd say, go for the inner solution if I were you – if you are going to depend on external things all stacking up correctly for you to be relaxed I reckon you are setting yourself up for a battering, whereas if you relax within yourself that will often help carry you through tricky external situations.

Thinking about this practically, it might be worth monitoring your breathing and noticing what is going on. Ideally I'd say that you want to be breathing deeply into your stomach, not shallow breaths in to the top of your lungs. What I do is if I ever find myself shallow breathing then I make a conscious effort to change to a deeper, slower breath. Like I have already said, I am certain horses clock this, and for you, what might start as a bit of a task can over the years become a very profitable and almost unconscious habit.

54

A lot of people who get serious about riding horses often
also develop an interest in martial arts. I do find that link quite
interesting, although the martial arts thing is not an avenue I have
pursued myself. There are strong links between balance, breath,
stability, the centre of your being, a calm and focussed mind, and
also something I haven't mentioned yet, being here now. All of these
things are extremely relevant to working with horses. I think that is
why, when I first came across Baucher, I felt a strong affinity to his
work. Remember back to the story of Molly and how we struggled
so much to get her back into the moment. And now, whenever I
work with the horse's mouth I am really aware of how focussed,
peaceful and present the horse becomes. It is very powerful stuff.
And what it most definitely is not is some little trick on the side
that might help sort out a few difficulties.

Ok, the last thing I want to talk about concerning sitting on a
horse is the need to be able to sit in a reasonably stable way. In
some forms of riding you can use the rein contact with the horse's
mouth to help you balance, but if you want to ride in the way I am
writing about here, where the communication between your hands,
through the reins to the horse's mouth is all done very precisely
and in softness, it is crucial that you don't suddenly need to use the
horse's mouth to stabilise your position.

What you need is what some people call 'an independent seat'.
I was once talking to a rider who religiously went every week
to have a one-hour lesson on seat training. He rode around and
around on the lunge while his teacher corrected his position and
helped him work on improving his seat. At the time I thought, 'Nah,
I wouldn't do that', and I haven't changed my view. If you want to
improve your seat, relax, sit in balance, and do what I do actually,
ride over very rough ground looking for your cows. Over the years
you will feel things improving. I can remember sitting on my horse
and not knowing what I was supposed to be feeling underneath
me. Now, when I get on I often feel that I am perfectly relaxed

How to sit on the horse

and comfortably moulded to my horse. It's a good feeling and I am certain my horse appreciates it too.

Another important point is to ride at a level that you are comfortable with and where you know that you have a very good chance of not compromising your horse's mouth through losing your balance. So for example you won't find me galloping across the moor jumping stone walls – not by choice anyway. I would also say here, and this is important too, riding in this way has no limitations – if anything I'd say it opens up horizons. You are riding the horse in the way that he was designed to go – how can anything be better than that. If you ever get a chance to read Captain Beudant's book, first published in 1931, then you will see what I mean.

6 WEIGHT-BEARING POSTURE, NECK EXTENSION AND GOING FORWARDS

One of the universal truths about horses is that if they don't carry the load of the rider correctly then sooner rather than later their backs will give out. Another truth is that the horses themselves do not have any idea about this, and another truth is nor do many people. There is now a massive industry built around treating the horses physical wellbeing and it is an almost accepted fact that your horse will need regular treatments from equine body workers.

If you ride your horse correctly and explain to him how to bear the weight in the correct way, then you, and more importantly your horse, can be freed from the often hugely expensive syndrome of endless treatments. Or to put it another way, the need for endless treatments is a direct result of insufficient knowledge and incorrect riding. Or to put it another way, ride your horse correctly, save him a load of pain and save yourself a load of money.

This is a huge subject but for the purposes of this book I am going to attempt to keep it simple. If you are interested in finding out more details, the whole thing is well documented elsewhere, and as far as I know is not in much dispute. For the horse's back to carry the weight of a human being his spine must be free from restriction, and he must be trained to use his abdominal and shoulder muscles to maintain the correct posture of his spine.

I actually see the whole thing in terms of every vertebra in the spine needing to maintain approximately even and parallel spacing with its neighbouring vertebras. Obviously I am not talking about this as an absolute rule because that would mean the spine couldn't bend at all. What I am saying is that there should not be prolonged periods of time when the spine is operating under duress, either from the use of human force or because of incorrect postural training. What I actually visualise when I see the horse being ridden are the vertebras in the spine and how they are lining up in relation to each other. It is very clear to me when there is pressure or strain at any point.

Let's just run through a few examples of how people inflict strain on a horse's spine. All of these examples, without fail, will have a detrimental effect on your horse's health and wellbeing.

- The horse sagging under the weight of his rider
- The horse being pulled in at the front – broken poll
- The horse with his head in the air
- The horse with strung out neck and not lifting up at the withers
- The horse overbending
- The horse getting back behind the bit – short neck

The horse must be allowed to travel correctly and in freedom.

Ok, there are a couple of things you need to know about horse anatomy to really understand how this all works. Firstly you need to know that the horse's front legs are not connected by any bone joints to his body. They are connected by muscles. If you bury a dead horse and dig him up in a couple of year's time, his front legs will be completely separate from his body. So here is a useful tip. If you are selling a horse and your potential buyer is concerned about the horse's height (measured at the wither), if you want him to be higher just lift his head up, and if you want him to be lower just lower his head. The front end of his body goes up and down between his front legs.

This is a really important fact, because if you remember back to all the stuff about balance, well, this is how you can affect it. By lifting or lowering your horse at the front you can transfer his weight from front to back or vice versa. By training your horse to raise his withers, in freedom and in balance, you are making a really good start on getting your horse to travel with a correct and healthy posture.

Weight-bearing posture, neck extension and going forwards

The second important fact that you need to know is that the horse's pelvis can actually kind of tuck under the horse sort of bringing the hind feet more under the horse and less trailing out of the back end. There are many expert horse people who are happy to debate the relevance of this, and to debate the terminology too. All I am going to say here (partly to avoid the risk of saying something really dumb) is that by asking your horse to work in balance, which encourages that 'tip' in the pelvis, over a period of time you will begin to feel a big difference to the way that your horse travels. I'm going to describe it like this – if you are asking your horse to step up a bank, say a couple of feet high, he could kind of drag himself up there using his front legs, or he could get his front legs up there and then push himself up the rest of the way with his hind legs. That's the difference I felt – my horse began to feel much more ready to use his back end in that way, and I have to say that my opinion is that that is a much healthier and effective way for the horse to work.

By practising riding your horse in freedom and in balance you begin to unlock the power that exists in your horse's back end. By allowing and training your horse to use his back end in this way you are making a really good start on maintaining and preserving the health of your horse's back.

I'll say right out front, if you try and do any of this with force, just forget it – it's not going to work. At best you are going to create a lookey-likey horse, but somewhere for sure, you (and your horse) will be paying the price. And at worst you will completely ruin your horse physically, and totally confuse and screw him up mentally, absolutely guaranteed. Do it properly – it's not that hard! I actually think the hardest part for most of us is letting go of all the crap we have picked up along the way. The actual work we are talking about here is pretty simple, as I hope you are beginning to see.

One thing that happens to me, a lot, is that I learn by my mistakes. I don't like being told what to do, or being told how things work.

Weight-bearing posture, neck extension and going forwards

I like to work things out for myself. I have lost my trust by being told so much stuff that later turned out to be crap. I do spend a lot of time re-inventing the wheel. But in defence of re-inventing the wheel, when I do eventually work something out I do tend to understand it quite well. And I also tend to be quite familiar with all the blind alleys, etc, that I find myself going up while I am spending all that time working things out.

I was so excited when I first glimpsed the power of balance. It tied in with all my desires to ride my horse in freedom. I spent hours hidden away in the indoor school practising balancing my horse. First I worked on halt to walk, and walk to halt. Then backing up, then going around corners, and then going sideways and on and on I went just adding in this move and that move – it was really good fun. And then one day my wife pointed out to me that what I was doing was all very well but I was scrunching my horse up at the front. I was horrified. In fact I was horrified to such an extent I didn't ride for a month. I couldn't work out how that was happening. I thought my horse was perfectly happy with the bit in his mouth and that as far as I could tell everything was fine. Now I know that I was scrunching him up, and actually sometimes now, if I watch videos of other riders practising riding in this way, I can see it is happening to some of them too.

So here is the answer to this problem. We have to get our horses to relax and extend their necks whenever we ask them too. By teaching your horse to lift up at the withers and then to extend his neck we can encourage him to be even happier with the bit, to such an extent that the 'scrunch' will become a thing of the past.

Stand by the side of your horse and take hold of the reins as if you are ready to do the flexions. Now ask your horse to give his mouth, and then lift his head, just a wee bit higher than he is comfortable with. Then take the outside rein and put a little bit more contact on it than you would maybe want to. As soon as your horse makes any attempt to drop his head, release the contact and allow him to drop his head. After you have done this a few times your horse will get the idea that as soon as he feels the outside rein he needs to drop his head and follow the bit downwards (I think this may be what conventional riders call, 'seeking the bit', but I'm not sure). Don't forget, as with all your cues, make sure you fade them as your horse learns them, so what maybe starts out as more than you would want to use, soon becomes almost less than you can feel. Practise this for a few days until it becomes really smooth, and make sure that you can get your horse to just follow the bit, not push on it. So for example if you just want your horse to extend his neck down for a few inches he should do just that, and no more.

The plan is that your horse becomes so happy with the feel of the bit in his mouth that wherever that bit goes he is absolutely happy to follow it, so that when he feels the bit going away from him he is happy to follow it until you say, 'That's fine boy, just there ok'. And that's how you get rid of the scrunch. It's possibly the hardest part of the whole job, but hang in there because it does complete things nicely. You now have a horse that, through his understanding of the bit, you can help him to understand how he should carry a rider in order to maintain a healthy back. Not only that, you also have a horse that you can train to give you the maximum comfortable ride that he possibly can.

And even more important than both those things, if you ask your horse to move forward with any speed, extending his neck is exactly what he would naturally do to do that. For the horse to move forward when he is restricted in the neck, either through force or through bad training, is going to be detrimental to both his health and performance.

Just to recap slightly here, once you have the neck extension working well from the ground in halt, then practise getting it working nicely on the move. Once that is working well, then practise it while riding the horse. Try in halt first and then on the move. Sometimes it is easier to get established in trot and sometimes in walk – you will have to experiment to work this all out. This can be a bit tricky – as I said earlier, I reckon this can be the trickiest part of the job. But keep on trying – it has to be done and it will come, and for sure you (and your horse) will feel the difference when it does.

7 LIFTING THE HORSE'S HEAD AND NECK

Controversy will always follow success, and sure enough it did for Baucher. In the European equestrian circles of the 1840s the debates and rivalries surrounding his work were intense. Baucher longed for acceptance of his work from the military, but after many mostly very successful attempts, it was not forthcoming. Nowadays the trainers that have embraced Baucher's work find themselves similarly surrounded by controversy. In this chapter I am going to try and explain one of the main reasons behind the controversy.

We had been working down in the school for about thirty minutes. Kate was riding an old thoroughbred mare and things were looking pretty good. The mare had a long history of a poor relationship with the bit and had got into the habit of travelling along in an inverted shape. I was standing on the sidelines looking at the mare and to be honest she was going along pretty nicely in walk. She was happy to take the bit forward, relax her back and use her abs to carry her rider. Then Sarah said to Kate, 'Shall we try a bit of trot and see what we've got there.'

Kate set the horse off in trot and the mare immediately raised her head and hollowed her back. I have to say (and I'm not for a moment saying this is right or wrong), I immediately thought, 'Oh god, let's not bother with this old mare – we've got loads of younger horses out there that would benefit twice as much from our time.' But then I thought, 'Mmmmm, let's just give it a minute or so and see which way the wind's blowing.'

So how do you get a horse to understand that the most beneficial way of going when you are in trot is to adopt the correct weight-bearing posture; that is to relax the neck, take the bit forward, soften the back and carry the person using the abs. It's more comfortable for the horse, and the rider, and it will give the horse a chance of staying sound and useful for longer. So in the case of this old thoroughbred, when she lifted her head we lifted the bit with it. Lifting the bit involves raising the hands in synch with her head, and as she offers to come down from the high

63

Lifting the horse's head and neck

position we lower our hands and allow the horse to take the bit forwards and down (neck extension). We are not saying anything to the mare using any heavy pressure, we're just saying to her, if you want to travel up here then that's fine but actually you will find it is far better to travel lower and longer. In a way, we are setting up the opportunity for her to work it out.

Anyway, Kate is riding around the school and the horse is half getting the idea and half not getting it. And I'm thinking, 'Well, this is pretty good really, at least she's getting it some of the time.' A really good tip to remember here, is when you are working with horses, if you can get one second of something then you can almost certainly get two, and so on and so on. And then it happened. Just as the horse raised her head and Kate raised her hands, into the school walked a well-known local trainer. 'Oh my god, what are you doing with your hands in the air like that?' she asked.

Uh oh, here I was in my very worst situation – talk about die of embarrassment – I would love never to see another person ever sometimes. I'll tell you what, how about this for an idea: I'll train my horse and you can come and see him when he's done, ok? What I really don't need ever, is someone coming along whose ideas about horse training are just about 180 degrees opposite to mine, and then asking me to explain why I am involved in something that is so contrary to what they think needs to be happening. You're lifting a horse's head to get it lower – why don't you just pull it down. So there you have it, lifting the horse's head is, as far as I can see anyway, one of the most controversial and difficult things for people to accept about Baucher's work. I think that was the case over 150 years ago and I think it's still the case today.

The controversy around this is why I am now going to have a go at explaining when to lift a horse's head and when not to, and how to do this correctly. There is no doubt, and I have heard the stories myself, there is a long catalogue of disasters caused by people doing this work incorrectly. It's hardly surprising really – all we've had to go on are books, and to be honest until very recently, not very clear books at that. I would say that without a fair amount of experience in understanding how to build in correct responses using feel and timing, you wouldn't stand a chance of getting this right. And I don't mean to sound arrogant there – I

64

hope and pray that I am not that way. I'll tell you one thing for free: I have made loads of mistakes along the way and no doubt will continue to do so. That's called learning.

When you pick up your horse's reins you need to have the correct response to them. It has to be clear in your mind and the mind of your horse. If you are asking in one way but getting two different responses then you need to sort that out. If you are asking for two different things but only asking in one way you need to sort that out too.

Let's look at an example. I really enjoy messing about sitting on my horse and just working on moving the feet around in different directions. So one thing my horses are usually pretty good at is backing up. So this is how I back up (and I know this is different to how a lot of people back up, but right now I don't want to get too involved in that, later maybe), I balance my horse up and then kind of roll her backwards by moving backwards myself. I remember years ago, I heard Mark saying that sitting on his horse was like sitting on a ball – he could roll him in any direction he wanted to go. I thought at the time, 'Wow, that sounds really cool!' well now I know what he meant, or at least I think I do anyway.

To do this it is important that when I pick up the rein to balance my horse I need a very specific response. I actually need my horse to stay in one piece. I'm not sure if that is an accepted horsey term or just something I have invented because it's what it actually feels like, so I'll explain it a bit more. I am looking for my horse's mouth to be totally happy with the feel of the bit and in no way to move away from it. So when I ask her to lighten up at the front and transfer some weight to the back, by lifting the bit, I need her to do it in one piece – I don't want her to make any major adjustments to her posture – I want her to adjust her balance by raising the base of her neck.

You may well get some different responses here, and I know this because I have got these responses too, you may get the horse

Lifting the horse's head and neck

lifting her head and stretching her neck high and hollowing her back. Or you may get a tuck under where the horse gives at the poll and curls up. You might get a pull down or even a pull up on the bit, or you may get a strong push out front. All of these responses are ways the horse has developed to deal with the bit, either because he is not happy with the bit, or because he thinks that is actually what you want. When I come across these different responses, what I would call 'incorrect' responses, I am very careful to make sure that my horse knows exactly what response I am looking for when I pick up my reins. I am looking for a soft relaxed mouth, a soft relaxed neck and a willingness to follow the bit, as one.

This is how I train my horse to have the response that I want to me picking up the reins and asking him to balance up. It is very simple but it can be quite difficult – does that sound familiar.?

Sit on your horse and gently pick up the reins and ask your horse for a soft mouth. Then ask him to rebalance his weight slightly off his front end onto his back end. If you get any response other than a gentle rebalancing, that is, if you get any change in head and neck posture, you need to work on explaining to the horse that that is not what you want. So for example, if my horse tucks under by breaking at the poll I would just lift him up from that straightaway and ask again for what I want. He will soon get the idea that I am not looking for the tuck under, so he may then try something else, for example he may try lifting his head. I don't want that either so as soon as he lifts his head I would just make that a slight hassle to him by lifting my hands so that the bit follows him upwards. As soon as he thinks about bringing his head down I would reward him with a nice soft release back down to his natural position. Then I'd ask again for what I want, and maybe he will keep trying the things he is used to doing for a few more times until he works out that they aren't really working for him anymore, and then he will start to try looking for alternatives. If he tries anything slightly in the region of what I do want, which is a nice soft rebalance, then I make sure everything is really nice and soft for him so that he begins to get an idea that he is going in the right direction. Now, if I do get in a real jam with this, sometimes I will help my horse realise what I am actually after by lifting him higher until he feels his balance tip back. After doing that a couple of times and giving him the release on the re-balance, he will soon get the idea that re-balancing is the job and that all the rest of his efforts are not what I am looking for. Of course I am then doubly careful to make sure that he doesn't start to think that lifting his head high is part of what I am looking for in the re-balance.

I feel like I need to stress this one more time – you must ensure that the initial response is the correct one. If re-balancing is what you are looking for, then you are not looking for it after your horse has put his head in the air, or tucked his chin under, or any other extra action he may want to throw in to the deal. You are looking for him to remain in a naturally comfortable position, stay soft and relaxed, and re-balance – that is all. If you think back to getting a C1 bend on cue, it is the same deal. You want just that, a simple C1 bend. You are not looking for a bend at the base of the neck, or a tilt on C2, or a shuffling of weight from shoulder to shoulder. You just want a simple, soft and relaxed C1 bend and as much or as little of a bend as you ask for. Precision counts for a lot for your horse.

I am going to go through the four basic responses to the bit that you are likely to get from your horse, and try to explain how I would deal with them. But before I do that I want to make clear how important it is that you try to understand the basic principles of the job you are trying to put in place with your horse. By doing this you can really help yourself avoid making big mistakes with your horsemanship, and some of these mistakes can be a bit crucial. But don't for one minute think that the mistakes you might make are anywhere near those that the vast majority of horse people are making anyway. Think about all the hideous restrictive tack, the awful bridling arrangements, leveraged bits, horrendous lungeing equipment and just plain bad horsemanship that most horses get subjected to, and then compare that to our aim of training our horse to willingly carry us correctly. With a little bit of care on our part there is very little chance that we will get anywhere near the ugliness of so-called modern horse training.

If we understand how the horse's body needs to operate in order to carry us comfortably and without excess strain, then that in itself will stop us from straying into areas where we might damage our horse. Remember, the horse can't work this out for himself. Of course some horses, and some breeds of horses are better designed than others for this job, to such an extent with a few horses you would actively have to train them to travel incorrectly ('Why not get one of those then?' I hear you say, and then you'd hear me say 'Yep, good idea.')

Similarly if we understand the psychology of the horse and we understand the freedom that a horse needs to feel in order to enjoy a sound mind, then that understanding in itself will prevent us from straying into areas where we will confuse and damage our horse's mental state. What I am saying here is that it is important we have some grasp of the whys and wherefores of what we are doing.

Ok, what is the plan if you have a horse who leans on the bit? This is the most likely scenario of all with older horses because so many of them have found this to be a successful way of dealing with our demands. With younger horses it is a relatively simple job to just say no, don't do that. I would do it very early on as soon as my horse is comfortable with the bit in his mouth, if I even feel so much as the smallest lean I would just vibrate the bit a little to show the horse that leaning is not a comfortable option. That, combined with the fact that there is no part of my training programme where I need my horse to lean, would be enough for it never ever to be a problem for my baby horse.

With an older horse who has been taught to lean, either inadvertently or on purpose, then things can get difficult, but not always so. There are several things I would try, and between them I would hope that the lean would quickly become a thing of the past. Firstly I would work hard on getting my CI bend. I would also practise standing in front of the horse and lifting his head with my hands either side of the bit. Now then, this is another situation where I may find myself lifting the horse's head higher, because there will be a point where he quits leaning on the bit. At first this may look a bit of a strain for him because he may invert his neck and back rather than adjust his balance, but it will come good by working with care. Once I have him able to walk around with me holding the bit, with him in balance and without any leaning, then I would work on replicating this while riding him.

An important point to notice here is that in order for your horse to lift his head he has to open his poll. In a leaning horse (a horse that pushes down on the bit) this is the opposite to what he has been practising. He has been locking his poll and pushing into the bit. That lock in the poll is a brace and you are looking to free that up. You need that poll joint to be free and easy – remember, tension and balance are not friends.

This kind of work really teaches you a lot about balance, because at first you may well find that your horse will only be able to avoid leaning when he is travelling relatively high and then only for short spells. If you up the speed, his centre of gravity will move forward and down and he will simply lose his balance. It may take some time to get to a point where he can carry himself at anything more than a slow high walk. In fact, I have to be honest here, I have given up on one horse because it was beginning to seem like he simply could not let go of his established means of going, which I have to say involved the heaviest lean you could ever imagine. I did get him going along in balance in a slow walk but as soon as I asked for more it all just fell apart. Of course that doesn't mean it was an impossible job, it possibly means I just wasn't good enough to do it, but sometimes it does get to a point where I just think, 'Nah, put that horse back out in the field'. I'd better just say here, that doesn't

happen often with me, I am not known for quitting, but there you go
– it does happen.

Let's take a closer look at working with the leaning horse. You
will probably find that when you balance him up and then ask him
to walk forward, his first steps will include a massive downwards
movement and transference of weight onto the front feet. You need
to tell him that isn't what you are looking for. The way I would do
that is as he begins the weight transfer I would stop him and re-
balance him, and then start again. After a few goes he will get the
idea that the forwards and down idea is not what you are after. It
might well feel as if you are asking him for something he has never
done – that may be the case, although I imagine that out in the field
he's gone forward in balance at some time in his life. When he finally
makes the first step in balance let him know he's got that just right.
The way that I work is when my horse cottons on to a new idea
that I am trying to show him, I repeat it a couple of times so that I
am pretty sure he knows the deal, and then I either quit the session
or move on to something else.

Typically, if I am doing a job similar to the above, I would get a few
'departures' in balance, try and hold the balance for a few steps, and
if all is going well, call it a day. I never bang on and on at anything
with my horse. Literally, just get the idea and move on.

Now, what about the horse that doesn't so much push down,
but pushes out front. In other words this horse locks his poll in
an open position? Again, work on the C1 joint. When that is really
good you will have so much more chance of freeing that poll joint.
In really difficult situations I would go for helping the horse give up
that pushing forward brace in the same way that I used to teach my
horses to give at the poll. But now I am really careful about making
sure that I don't leave the horse the impression that the bit is
something to get behind.

So how to break that forward pushing brace. I would stand to
one side of the horse's head and hold the reins about six inches

from the bit. Then I would ask for the soft mouth, and when that comes through nicely, just ask the horse to give at the poll by moving the bit gently towards his chest. At this point he is likely to do one or both of the following. He will push forward against your ask, and/or go backwards to avoid the ask. My response to both of these re-actions is to quietly continue to ask for what I want, which is a give at the poll.

Let's look more closely at what is happening – it might be helpful if I can describe just how much pressure and what response is involved here. Bear in mind that this is me and my work – with someone else it may be different. So I try to remain constant in my ask, but the horse may vary his response. If he really pushes then there will be more pressure. In fact the pressure will be governed by the horse. This is my understanding of Baucherism in a nutshell really. Oppose all resistances. This is now pretty much my complete approach to horsemanship.

There will come a point, sooner or later, where the horse, if his plans aren't working out, will try something different. His new idea may not be what I want, so then I hang in there until he tries something else. He may try swinging around, or throwing his head, or backing up really fast, or anything else that comes into his head, but eventually he will try something roughly in the direction of what I want. And then he will automatically find a release. It works almost without my input and the timing will be perfect. With a few repeats, before long that first small feeling of release will build in the horse's mind into the obvious solution and the job will be done.

So at risk of repeating myself here, with this particular brace, work hard on getting the lateral flexions really good – that may lead to success on its own, but if you end up having to deal head on with the problem be really careful not to teach the horse to back off the bit.

'You know that thing that you did with Gloria's horse?' said the voice on the phone.

'You'll just have to give me a bit more information than that' I replied.

Lifting the horse's head and neck

'Well, since you did that she's been winning all her dressage competitions'.

Oh my god, how my heart sank. I remembered back a few months to working with Gloria's horse. I had spent quite a while getting her to give up pushing forwards onto the bit. It had worked really well and I had explained to Gloria that she needed to be really careful now, not to have her horse pulling back behind the bit.

'Yes, she has been fantastic. So light in the hand and she looks so beautiful,' Gloria's Mum continued. 'The only thing is it's gone wrong again. She's gone back how she used to be, so can I bring her over and you do it again?'

I knew what was happening, in fact I had set my own horse up that way many years ago, and it did work well, but now I know that it isn't correct. And as for winning at dressage, well, that's what really got to me. I imagined the judges fixating on the horse's broken poll and thinking 'Mmmmmm, that is a nice horse.' Well, she is a nice horse, but it's so wrong to look at isolated parts of the horse. Just because the horse's head is vertical doesn't mean the horse is going correctly – in fact in this case it is definitely not. To be behind the bit like that requires tension in the neck. It absolutely is not the same as total relaxation of the mouth on the bit. And aside from that you have also lost the feel of the horse in your hands – she just is not there.

That's just a little story to encourage you to be careful if you go down the road of breaking the brace in the horse's poll.

And then we come to the horse that pushes up on the bit. The first time that I felt this I was really surprised. See the thing is I was travelling into unknown territory, and without a guide too. This little horse was clearly not happy with his mouth and when I got hold of the bit I felt this huge and constant upward push. There were a few people around and I didn't want to say, 'Ooooh I've never come across this before', so I just thought, 'well, have some belief here, surely what I have to do is resist the pressure'. So I was gently holding the bit either side of the horse's mouth and the pressure that I was feeling from the horse was quite strongly upwards in my hands. I firmed up my hands so that the horse couldn't just push the bit out of his way, and fair do's, he was a bit surprised by this and made a few efforts, some quite dramatic, to shove his way through my hands. But I remained firm, with loads of softness there whenever the horse wasn't pushing against me. It did take a while but eventually he worked out that the whole thing was much more comfortable if he just relaxed and accepted that the bit needed to be just sitting there quietly in his mouth. I guess one way of looking at it is that the horse had got his mouth in neutral – his mouth wasn't re-acting to the bit, it was accepting it.

From there it didn't take long before I had the little horse travelling along with the bit sitting quietly in his mouth too. So then we put the rider on. He was a young friend of mine called Donald, about thirteen years old, but anyone could see that he was a master horseman in the making. Up he jumped and off he went, and it was beautiful. The flexions were working smoothly, the bit was quiet in the mouth, and I said to Donald, 'Balance that horse up', and he did, and I guess I smiled, well actually, I know I did.

And the fourth response you might get from the horse to the bit is the horse that gets behind it. This was the situation that I was in with Splash. So how are we going to deal with that? Looking back I actually found this quite easy at the time. Maybe I got lucky. Firstly work on the mouth. You need a nice reliable soft mouth on asking – this on its own is half the battle I reckon. Once the horse realises that you are looking for the soft mouth rather than for her to pull away from the bit the job is almost done.

Then get the flexions working really well, and if you are really beginning to get the hang of this now, go for getting the neck extension cue in there too. Get all this working nicely with you using the reins while you walk alongside your horse. You will feel her standing up nice and straight on the corners too if it is all going well. And then get on and see what you have got. See if your horse

Lifting the horse's head and neck

will follow that bit while you're up there rather than pulling away from it. See the problem is that if your horse pulls back behind the bit you won't be able to do the flexions, because what will happen is she will kind of curl up trying to do what she thinks you want her too. She has to be comfortable with the contact of the bit in her mouth for all this to work.

So I'm not saying that I have covered everything there, what do I know! But the important thing is to be able to work out your response to whatever comes your way. And that is one of the joys of Baucherism – it makes it easy. Give equal resistance from you to any resistances and pressures that come from the horse to you, and you are always providing the opportunity for the horse to find the release. So let's imagine a completely mythical problem that you happen to come across in your horse. What if, when you pick up the bit, your horse twists his head anti-clockwise, glazes over, and pulls backwards. Now, I've never had that happen to me myself, but it wouldn't worry me if it did. All I would do is resist, and if the glazing over was persistent, I would wake him up maybe by vibrating the bit or tapping him on the leg, make sure he is present, and wait for him to work out that his actions weren't that beneficial and see if I could hang in there long enough to help him find something in the direction I wanted him to look for.

Again always remember, if you can get one second of what you want, you can almost certainly get two.

8 IS YOUR HORSE STRAIGHT?

Now, I'm pretty sure that most of the people reading this book will almost certainly have heard the word 'straightness' in relation to horses. I remember reading how important it was for the rider to sit straight, and I'm pretty sure I have read somewhere, or been told, that if my horse isn't straight it's because I'm not straight. That my dear friends is – and I'm probably not allowed to swear, so what I shall say is – that my friends is total nonsense.

Straightness in horses is no more than a natural propensity for them to prefer one side or the other, much the same as we are either right or left handed. I don't want to spend too much time discussing this, but it is quite important to at least accept it as a fact. If you watch a foal with its mother you will see that it will be more inclined to drink from one side than the other. If you work with youngsters you will almost certainly see that they feel safer with you on one side than the other. And once you start getting used to seeing straightness, or more accurately non-straightness, in the horse, you will see from how the horse is standing and moving just what the situation is re. left and right sidedness.

Let's go back and look more closely at the situation I was in with Splash. I could turn right no problem, but when I tried to turn left I had the problem of Splash turning through the shoulder rather than walking around the turn. Of course, at the time I didn't realise that that was what was happening – but now I do. So why did Splash fall through the shoulder, and why did she not want to bend her head to the left? Now, years later, the answer is obvious to me.

Splash is a right sided horse. She was not comfortable turning left. In animal behaviourist terms maybe they would say that when she needs to run for safety she's ready to go right. She is actually braced and set up to run that way. I am not exaggerating to say that I have seen some horses positively panic when I have been fairly insistent that I need them to give in the direction that they are uncomfortable with going. It is *a very big deal.*

Once I had begun to take on board the importance of all this to the horse, a whole lot of stuff began to fall into place for me. For example, I began to realise that I was often asking my horse to do things that she actually found quite scary, like going in a direction that made her feel quite vulnerable.

And then I started to tie the whole thing in with balance. I had already realised that riding in balance was having a profound experience on the state of mind of my horses, but now I was beginning to see why. An unbalanced horse is not going to feel so safe within himself, he is not so ready to run, as a balanced horse. I began to realise that if I wanted to ride horses it was my duty to train them to feel comfortable to work equally on both sides

So how can we add straightness as a quality into our horse – that is the question. Well, ironically (correct use of that word? – ironically I have no idea!), the way to put straightness into your horse is make sure he has no resistance to bend. If he is soft from head to tail then he won't be one-sided. He will surely always have a preference for one side or the other, but the more flexible horses become, the happier they are to travel straight.

Now that I am writing all this down I can see the simplicity of it all. It's actually all the same stuff. Here is the list of jobs we have to do.

1. Get a good leg cue working
2. Get the flexions working really well
3. Get your horse so he can walk in balance around corners
4. Get your horse so he can move sideways at the front end
5. Get your horse so he can move sideways at the back end

That might sound like a lot, and actually it can sometimes be quite difficult for people to piece it all together, but once you get your head around it, it is all a very logical and simple process. Obviously you can take things as far as you want to go. Personally if I can get that little list working in walk, I'd be thinking that's the basics in there, and from there it's going to be pretty straightforward for me to get my horse to how I want him to be. But for other people who want more performance from their horse, well, it's a good base for you to start from too. You can just take things as far as you want to go – there's no limit really. Once the basics are in the horse things can move forward pretty quickly – remember the story of Gericault.

So let's have a little look at the individual items on the list above.

Step 1 – Get a good leg cue working

I'm not sure if I have discussed the leg cue yet. This is important. Your horse needs to go when you ask, and he needs to go with some life, at the speed that you want him to go at. Actually, this applies to everything that you ask your horse to do – it's no good if it happens tomorrow. It needs to happen NOW and your horse needs to be happy coming through with it. This is just basic horsemanship really. But if you don't have that response built in to your horse you are not going to be able to get straightness. If you have to work to get your horse going, or you have to work to keep your horse going, then it simply isn't going to work.

So you're sitting on your horse and you want to go. You pick up the reins, and hopefully your horse realises you are about to ask him to do something. You ask him for his mouth. You sit in balance and gently touch with your legs, and off he should go. No hesitation, no reluctance, just go. And if there is any hesitation or reluctance, then you have to do something until it disappears. Do something – slap your leg, have a stick and hit your boot, anything really, but it has to get a result. You need to feel that horse surge forward so that he understands that that is what your lightest of leg cues means. And you do that every time until he goes forward with life, at your softest ask.

And then your horse also needs to know that that is what you want until you ask otherwise. If you are having to ask again for forward, or you are having to work hard yourself just to keep him going, well, I'm afraid straightness and balance are not going to be on the agenda.

That's just got me thinking about what if you have a horse situation where the leg cue works too well. Actually, that's not the correct wording is it – a horse that rushes off, or charges around way faster than what you want, is not really a leg cue problem. That is a 'lack of a soft horse' problem really. I would be working hard at improving the softness in the horse. Remember how to get a light horse soft – that's what you need to be working on there.

Step 2 – Get the flexions working really well
Your horse needs to be happy with the bit and have a nice soft mobile mouth. You need to have the flexions working nicely, and you need your horse to be happy to raise and lower his neck on demand. See chapters 1, 2 and 3.

Step 3 – Get your horse so he can balance around corners
Your horse needs to be able to walk around corners in both directions. Imagine the line of the corner – it might be a quarter of a 5m circle – he needs to be able to walk that line softly and in balance.

Step 4 – Get your horse so he can move sideways at the front end
Now, this is a big one. It will make a huge difference to lots of things, and it's fun. This is how I do it.

Get on your horse, and ride him down the side of the school and ask him to bend his neck at C1 towards the wall. At first he will probably think you are barmy asking him to turn into a wall, but when the penny drops he will realise that bend and turn are two different things. Again it's the same stuff here – as soon as he makes a little try, make sure the nice soft release is there and for the first few times just be satisfied with the smallest of tries. Before long

78

your horse will be able to travel straight along the side with a C1 bend to the wall.

When you have that well established you can go for your first turn through the shoulders. The fact is that the first time I consciously felt my horse move through the shoulder I was absolutely thrilled (cue here for advanced riders to yawn and sigh). So as you come up the side of the school, approaching the corner, ask for the C1 bend towards the wall. Balance up your horse front to back and try and lead your horse around the corner with your inside rein. At first he will probably wonder why you are crashing him into the end of the school, but if you persist he will work out that in order to get around the corner he needs to step over laterally, through the shoulder. If he's nicely balanced up this will all be quite easy.

Get that working well on one side and then get the other side done in the same way. I always find it very exciting at this point because I begin to realise that this is the start of me and my horse being able to do all kinds of movements. Once you have the corners down then the next step is to keep the cue for the shoulder move on and see if your horse can actually bring you off the wall. Get that working and it won't be long before you are trying for complete 180s away from the wall. And then you'll be trying for it with the back feet rooted – actually with the front to back balance in place you soon realise that anything and everything is possible – it's just down to work and dedication (sadly neither of which are my strongest suits). I'd better just point out here, and I have to say I don't know why but there is surely a good reason, people who do this stuff and who are seriously into more advanced riding don't really go in for lots of stationary moves like turn on the haunches and turn on the forehand. I think it probably hinders some of the work that they plan to do later on. But I just enjoy it a lot so that's what I do.

If you are finding this lateral move tricky here is a huge tip. As you come to the point where you want to ask the horse to move his

Is your horse straight?

front end sideways, make sure you and the horse are in balance and that you are carrying no tension within yourself. Do the whole thing quite slowly and keep the weight off the front end. Some people here would also say that it really helps if you use your weight to influence the direction here too. Personally I don't do that – it takes all my powers just to keep the whole outfit in balance – but I do understand that many riders eventually aim to ride their horses using weight cues and that is of course fine.

I'll just explain why the C1 bend in the opposite direction to the shoulder turn works so well. It's because the natural balance, when for instance, you turn the head right, is for the weight of the horse to move left. It makes the lateral step with the outside leg easy. This is the process of straightening your horse. Imagine now a horse that only wants to bend to the right. He is going to find it easy to move through the shoulder to the left, but difficult, if not impossible, to the right. If we can provide him with an exercise programme that helps balance both sides, which this exercise would obviously be part of, then we are well on the way to straightening our horse.

Step 5 – Get your horse so he can move sideways at the back end

Now we come to the last step. If you think about it it's the last part of the horse that you need to be able to control, or at least it is for my purposes. If I can get this in place then I can go forwards, backwards, move the front end sideways, move the back end sideways and move both ends sideways together. What more could I want!

The cue that I want to use for moving the backend sideways is ultimately, me turning my hips a little. So say I want to move the back end anti-clockwise, then that is the feel I would give the horse through my lower body. If you sit on a horse and rotate your hips anti-clockwise your left leg will move back slightly and if you keep going with that leg it will touch the horse. It's kind of common sense. Of course you could say, ah yes, but the right leg will move

80

forward too and push the front of the horse across too. Yes, that is right, and if you want to you can do that as well, but for me, I choose not to. I'm pretty precise with what I teach my horse, and I try to keep it simple too.

I do want to stress, you can use whatever cues or ways you like to move your horse however you want to move him – he is your horse. What I am writing about here is how I have worked out how I want to move my horse right now. It might change – that wouldn't matter to me at all – if I find a better way of doing something, or if I want to try out some other things to see how it goes, that is up to me.

I'll just explain why being able to move the back end laterally will help to straighten your horse. Pretty much every horse will be using each of their back legs differently – by that I mean pushing forward with more power in one leg than the other. Which leg is more powerful will depend on whether the horse is right or left sided. Once you can take the back end off the track, in other words have the horse travelling forwards on a diagonal, then you can put the horse in a situation where he will have to use his weaker leg more than his stronger one. By using this exercise you can even him up and help him work towards travelling straight.

I'm going to point something out here that may be helpful. And the reason I am going to say this now is because it was at this point that I really realised that my inhibitions about what I can and can't do with horses really made things difficult for me and my horse. I could not get Splash to move her back end over in response to my leg cue. I tried and I tried to the point where I nearly gave up. I even began to construct an argument to prove that it wasn't actually necessary to get that particular job done – Yes, I was getting desperate. The next day I tried again, but this time I was a bit more determined. I put my cue on, got no response, leant back and slapped her on the bum. She got a bit of a shock, but boy, she did move over. I had broken the brace. From there things just got easier for both of us. Did Splash care – nah, I don't think she gave a damn.

Is your horse straight?

In fact I'm certain that she was relieved to finally know what the hell I was asking for all that time.

What I am trying to say here is, if you can dump all your ideas about the hows, whys and wherefores of horse training, and also dump all your ideas about what is acceptable and what isn't – become free – then the whole job suddenly becomes a whole lot easier. If you are free to explain to the horse what you need him to do, and you are free to do whatever it takes to help him understand it, then things can happen pretty quickly. Because you are working without limitations everything is very clear to you and the horse. The job gets done more quickly and the horse understands it more clearly. You have the horse's attention, he is focussed, the response is installed, and you have a happier and far safer horse.

I'll just say also, if you don't fancy doing the above, you can easily do this by having a friend on the ground who helps explain to the horse what it is that you want when you put the cue on. You can use a flag or a rope to move her across – whatever. The important thing is that at the end of the day the horse 100% knows that when the cue comes on she moves across. End of job!

One day I was riding Splash in the indoor school. I spent a lot of time riding her in there because in there she wasn't scared and I wanted to really cement the responses to my cues into her so that when we went out, if things went haywire, I could use the responses to keep her with me – that was my plan anyway. Sarah was riding Molly and showing someone how to do some move or other. I was kind of half listening and I worked out, maybe wrongly, that what she was trying to explain was to get the horse to go around in a small circle with the front end on a smaller circle than the back end. Splash was pretty on form at that moment and I was feeling good too, so I thought I'd give it a go. We needed to move the front end in on each step and the back end out on each step. I'd never tried it before, so I balanced her up, slowed her right down and gave it a go. Wow, we could do! I've tried it a few times since

82

then – it's not something I find that easy but it's pretty good fun when it works.

The purpose of this story is to show that once you have the cues built in and functioning, and combine them with front to back balance, then you and your horse can work together as a team and do the exercises that will help to gymnasticise him and keep him healthy. I know that move I did is basic stuff to most horse people but for me it showed me the potential of what can be achieved if things are explained clearly and correctly to the horse. I also know that vast numbers of horse riders use tack combined with force to manoeuvre their horses through vastly more complicated routines than that. That, to me, is a completely pointless waste of time, and ugly in the extreme. But there you go – each to their own I guess.

9 TRAINING YOUR HORSE STEP-BY-STEP

Please re-consider the title of this book, 'Baucher and the Ordinary Horseman'. I am not an advanced horse person, and neither do I have any desire to be one. I'm hoping (and guessing) that there are many more of us out there who like working with horses and who are not overly ambitious, but who nevertheless are keen to find ways of making our work a pleasure for both ourselves and the horse. What makes work a pleasure for the horse? The horse needs to feel safe and in order to feel safe he needs to understand the situation. It is our responsibility to make sure that is what is happening.

Many years ago I took my place in the audience at my first Mark Rashid clinic. There were about thirty of us there and although I had read one of his books I really had no idea what to expect.

For me at that time, horsemanship was a pretty amorphous affair. It consisted of about ten years of almost total confusion followed by a couple of years where I began to feel that things were beginning to make a small amount of sense between me and the horse. However, I still carried with me a huge feeling of, how can I describe it, a sort of feeling of unravelling a huge mystery. It was exciting. It reminded me very much of how things were for me in my life in my late teens in the late 60s and early 70s. I felt as if I were picking away at the mystery of the universe and that slowly, very slowly I was beginning to reveal the answer of existence. Again, exciting times, but certainly not a story for this particular book.

So anyway, there I was sitting in the audience and Mark was there, messing around with his AV equipment. He had his cowboy gear on and everything he did seemed to me to be pretty quietly done and with a lot of focus. I was really looking forward to watching him work and about two minutes into him making a start I was hooked. At last I had found someone working with horses in a logical, explainable and non-mysterious way, and it all came with a total bonus – the horses got it too. And the nice thing is that I can easily tell you what it was that I liked about the way Mark worked, and also why I could immediately relate to it. The girl came into the school with her mare and the mare simply couldn't stand still on the end of the rope. So Mark took the rope and got that job done. Then when he went to lead the mare it had no idea about Mark's personal space, so he got that job done. Then he needed the mare to stop when he stopped, so he got that done, and so on. It wasn't long before the horse was going, 'this guy makes sense – I'm happy to hang out with him'.

Just one job at a time and get it done. Explain it to the horse so that the horse understands it, and when he gets it let him know he's got it, and then move on. Simple, it needs to be oh so simple. That must be ten years plus since I saw Mark do that, and since then I have worked hard at simplifying my act. And the simpler I can make it the better the horses like it. Nothing that you do with horses should be difficult or complicated. If it is then you are working further up the line than you should be – that's what I'd say anyway.

I remember watching owners coming into the school with their horses and being amazed that the trainer always seemed to know where to start. There must be some kind of knowledge that the trainer has that allows him to see where the horse is at, and then there must be some kind of system that the horse's situation fits right in to. It took me a while to figure it out, partly because nobody explained it to me, but maybe they did and I just didn't hear them. Or, and I think this is true, it is mostly because it is just one of those things that you really do have to figure out for yourself.

So here is the answer – I don't know if it will be of any help to you. It may be that you will have to work it out for yourself anyway and then, just like I did, you can say, 'Ah, now I get what you are talking about'.

The answer is that the first thing you need is a horse that is quiet, focussed, and willing to work for you. So there is the first job – get that in place. Once you have that set up then the next job is to teach the horse the correct way of carrying its rider. You can put this knowledge into the horse one step at a time. I'd almost go as far as to say that putting this info into the horse in any other way is going to be a tough and probably very hit and miss affair. I have heard people say that the horse will work this out for himself. That is absolutely not true. There are some horses that are so well bred that they can or do carry the rider correctly, but even in these cases it doesn't take much from the rider to stop that happening.

Think about the ground that we have covered in the first eight chapters of the book. It covers a series of steps that can each be established in the horse. I always think that if you get ahead of yourself here and rush to get to a certain point, you do run the risk of building on dodgy foundations. You will get caught out, for sure.

As you go along with this work you may begin to feel if there is something not quite right about the way a horse responds when you are with him. For example, you may feel crowded, or you may feel resistance in the rope. Anything at all that I feel that isn't how I want it to be, I try to deal with it there and then. I do this simply because I know that any confusion in the horse about the basic stuff will inevitably show up further down the line. Remember here, we are not talking about having a horse that we can hold together with force and tack – we are looking to have a horse that understands how we want him to be, to such an extent that he can be that way without any physical restraint. You simply cannot have a horse that suddenly decides to walk off, or do anything off his own bat at all really, so everything needs to be set up really well right from the start.

You may well ask what on earth has all this got to do with Baucherism and frankly you may be right. I think what I am talking about here is more about my own personal interpretation of Baucherism actually. For me I have come to see that everything that happens between me and the horse is about how I set things up in our relationship. I can choose how it is going to be. And my choice is that I don't want any resistances at all in my horse. So when I feel resistances I work to take them out. Any resistance that I feel, I oppose it until it has gone. That is my interpretation of Baucher's work.

I know that for several years I have been able to communicate quite nicely with horses using what, in the horse world, is called feel. But since I began to understand Baucherism I have also begun to understand feel. I noticed that the feel coming from my hands was different. It had changed, maybe only slightly, but that small change was huge in the effect that it was having on the horses. What brought about that change in me was my understanding of the need to oppose the resistances when I feel them. That alone has changed the feel in my hands.

❧

My friend Colette told me that she knew of a really good horse that needed a home. Now, I don't need a horse – I have too many already. But for some reason this one played on my mind. I made the fatal error of getting in touch with Jo, the owner, to ask her about the horse. Sure enough it wasn't long before I made Jo an offer and we reached a deal.

A few days later Dan arrived. He is a nicely built steely-grey cob-cross off Bodmin Moor. He is a beautiful looking horse. We chucked him in the field with a few other horses and that was that. There was the usual stuff from the wife, you know, 'what the hell did you get that horse for – he's just been in the field since he got here', that kind of stuff – nothing too serious. So one day I decided I'd better get Dan out of the field and see what he was like.

I went up to him and caught him fine. Then I went to the gate, opened it and walked through it. I'd not got far before I felt this huge tug on the lead rope. Dan didn't know how to follow the feel in the rope around a gate. He had never worked out that you need to stop, and move your back end around to stay with the handler. His method was to walk straight and have the handler shut the gate and then walk past him to carry on the journey.

Training your horse step-by-step

At first I thought, oh my god, I've bought a horse who can't step sideways. I know it sounds a bit naïve to think that thought but I've bought so many horses that turn out to have unforeseen setbacks I am always ready for the next one. I got the gate shut and stood there looking at Dan. Then I thought I'd better just check out that he can move sideways. At first he didn't know what I was on about, you know, new cues and so on, but we soon got it organised. So I tried the gate again. This time I was ready though. As he went to plough on his own sweet way I was careful to make sure that there was some firmness behind my softness. Dan felt the firmness and kind of pulled himself up and wondered what to do. I just stood there and waited to see if he could work out a solution. His head had come around a bit already because of the tight rope so it didn't take him long to work out that he needed to shift his back end around to get comfortable again.

So that's the difference in feel, right there – it has firmness behind it. And how far away from the firmness was the softness – no distance at all really, it is almost part of the same feeling. As long as Dan was concentrating, as soon as he felt the firmness coming into the rope he could feel the softness leaving. For me now, feel is like that all the time, and the horses soon learn to stay with it. It makes a huge difference to everything that we do. And to me, well, that is Baucherism. I sometimes watch people leading their horses and letting them walk through the feel they have in the rope. I cringe now when I see it – I'm afraid that, right there, they are teaching their horse everything that he doesn't need to know.

And here is the big big bonus to keeping the quality of true feel in your work – with almost all horses when they start to feel it in you they start to reflect it in themselves. The first time Dan went around that gate, for sure it felt a bit like a cargo ship turning in a rough sea, but a few times later he was flowing around it pretty nicely.

So there you have it really. If you can create a horse without resistances, from there you can build in to your horse whatever you want to, to be able to do whatever you want to do with him.

No longer is training the horse some slightly amorphous, slightly mystical, slightly hit and miss, slightly incomprehensible process that you can read about and study forever but never quite understand. It is now a clear, step by step process that not only makes sense to you, but also mentally and physically makes sense to your horse too.

10 'HAND WITHOUT LEGS, LEGS WITHOUT HAND'

I am going to dedicate this chapter to François Baucher.

Born in 1796, he spent his whole life exploring and developing his way of working with the horse. His methods were revolutionary and, on balance, during his life he probably had more detractors than supporters. Looking at the situation in today's terms I'd say that his main fan base were the ordinary people who enjoyed his circus performances and the ordinary soldiers who appreciated the difference that his ideas made to their horses. His main detractors were those in the established horse world who no doubt saw his work as a threat to their power. Baucher's work and his writings stirred up strong emotions.

1842 was an important year for Baucher, firstly with his tremendous performance with Gericault, and then the publication of his second book, which he called his 'New Principles'. On the back of this success Baucher was drafted in to help improve the horsemanship of the French cavalry and he proceeded to run several experiments with various regiments using his methods. There are many documented success stories of his efforts with the army, but behind the scenes things weren't going so well. The powers that be were not too happy about having such a controversial figure working under their authority. It wasn't long before he was sent on his way.

Disillusioned by so much rejection Baucher became despondent and went back to work with the travelling circus. Even then he continually ran into intense opposition. At one time he found a willing audience for his work in Germany, only to come up against the local riding authorities yet again.

Baucher returned to France, even more despondent about his work ever being appreciated by the powers that be. Back in Paris he continued his work at the circus. It was here, in 1855, that things took a very dramatic and unexpected turn. While working with a horse, a large chandelier fell from the circus roof and landed on him. Although he survived this terrible accident, on recovery he had virtually lost all the power of his legs. He was never able to ride in public again.

However, his injuries had a huge effect on his horsemanship. From this point on his work is described as 'Baucher's second manner'. It is this second manner that has loosely survived as Baucherism to this day. In fact I would say, for myself, it is the work that Baucher did after 1855 that really makes most sense to me. The saying, 'Hand without legs, legs without hand' comes from this era of Baucher's work. When I first heard that saying, it truly set bells ringing in my mind. Remember, for many many years I had been desperately struggling with the idea, that still prevails today, that somehow we can ask our horses to go forward with our legs while at the same time pulling them backwards with our hands. I thought it was nonsense then, but didn't have the balls to say so. Now I know it's nonsense, and I am more than happy to say so to anyone who wants to listen.

Baucher died in 1873. It was reported, by his student and friend, General L'Hotte, that his last words and actions were thus: 'Then taking my hand and giving it the position of the hand of the curb, he told me, "Remember well, always this", and he immobilised my hand under the pressure of his – "Never that" and he drew my hand nearer my chest.'

That last sentence may seem a little confusing. But to me it means so much. Firstly, the simple thing is to have no backward pull in the hand. That's not so easy if you have been practising pulling all your life. I think of it as forces. Can you cancel out the force of a pull from your horse without pulling back? Of course you can – just present him with a solid feel. Ironically trying to cancel out a pull from your horse by pulling back is for sure just going to make the situation so much worse. Horses struggle to weigh up a pull, they

'Hand without legs, legs without hand'

almost always pull against it, but they understand a fixed hand. Truth be told, horses are the true Baucherists around here – that's how they operate, and I guess that's why it works so well for us when we begin to understand what Baucherism is.

Now having read the above paragraph, hopefully it helps makes sense of the phrase, 'he immobilised my hand under the pressure of his'. It's about forces – equal opposition to forces – that is my understanding of Baucherism.

Anyway, good luck with all this. I openly admit I have strayed a long way from the more conventional interpretation of Baucher's work. I believe my straying has happened for good reason. By studying and practising Baucher's work, the way that I am with my horses has changed so much for the better. My horses' understanding of me is now so much better. Although I clearly wasn't a terrible horseman before I came across Baucher, I have to say that the change in the feel in my hands (and my whole being actually) has made me even less of a terrible horseman now. That change, above all, is what I value more than the rest of the stuff put together. In fact I'd say there is a pretty good chance that if you can get that feel sorted out, the rest of the stuff will certainly follow along much more easily.

11 SYSTEMS, TEACHERS, HORSE-TRAINER SPEAK, AND YOU

Now we come to the final aspect of my take on Baucherism. And this is the part of it that I really like, to the point where I almost get excited by it (but not quite). Here it is. Once you have understood the basic principle of the philosophy, ie, understand that the aim is to meet resistance with an equal and opposite resistance, then from there, from that point on, you are your own teacher. Just think of the time and money that you are going to save, never mind all the excruciating situations that you end up in by desperately trying to work out what it is that you need to do next to understand the mystery of horsemanship.

Just to qualify that a little – I am not saying that you only need to know this one small thing. What I am saying is that actually you need to know a whole lot more than that, but with that one small thing to help you, you are now in a position to be able to use your overall knowledge to help make your horse into a really good horse.

And just to qualify that a little bit more, I am not talking about meeting massive force from the horse with massive force from you. That will almost certainly end in disaster. This is about making the judgement of where you can safely meet the horse and begin to explain to him as quietly as possible that this is how you want things to be set up. If you have a wild horse on your hands it may be that the most that you can get from him in the first session is for him to understand that you would prefer it if he didn't try and drive you out of the field. You know, can you reach some kind of agreement with him so that you can both stay there in that space.

We have to try to use common sense at all times, and try not to be dogmatic in the theory and practise of our horsemanship. Above all stay safe, unless you prefer it otherwise!

လ

Systems, teachers, horse-trainer speak, and you

So as I have already said, maybe even a few times, over the years I have fought pretty hard against using systems in my horse work. I have watched so many horses come unstuck by people adhering to the totally inappropriate rules of whichever particular system they happen to be subscribing to. I'm not sure if I was convinced that there would be some small thing, that if you knew it, it would sort out every problem that you may come across with your horse. I think the truth is more that is what I hoped would be the case. And many trainers have made, and continue to make, good careers by selling this or that particular method – you know the sort of thing, 'yes, if you do this it will resolve every situation'.

The horse world can be a mighty complicated place. There are a lot of people with a lot of different ideas about horses and how things should be done between us and them. Some people have a huge moral take on it all too. In fact over the last thirty or so years practically a whole new language has grown up around the horse. New words have come into use to describe more clearly what it is that is going on.

One of the first new words I came across all those years ago was 'start', as in 'We are not going to break in the horse, we are going to start him'. I went along with that for years, but now, taking a closer look at it, I almost wish I hadn't. You see, people didn't like the image of a horse being broken. People really wanted to think that we can work on this together, man and horse. We should be a partnership, or a team. And anyway, it is surely obvious that the horse will work better for us if he is a willing partner in all that we do.

That all sounds really good doesn't it? And in a way I don't disagree with it. But from there we have invented a whole new way of looking at horses. Very soon we were using little phrases such as 'Give the horse a choice' and 'Make it the horse's idea'. Phrases that actually when you think about them, they do sound really good, but at the same time they are hugely open to interpretation.

And as a result of this kind of 'cultural shift' in our approach to the horse, it actually became almost wrong to tell the horse what to do. We could, at a pinch, ask the horse, but whatever we do we really shouldn't tell him. What we were really looking for was some kind of undefined method of communication that somehow allowed us to work together and get things done. I won't lie, I bought into this as much as the next guy, but as time went by and my understanding of what the horse wanted out of the deal became clearer, I began to see what a blessed relief it was to the horse when I just said, 'Do this'. As long as he knew what I was on about he was just fine with that arrangement.

I then began to look more closely at what was really going on, and I began to see that an awful lot of us were saying one thing but actually doing another. I don't think we were doing this on purpose. It was purely as a result of almost what you might call 'commercial pressure'. If you are a reasonable horse trainer and you are looking for clients, you are obviously going to attract more business if you use words and phrases that make you appear to be more sensitive to the horse's needs (and feelings). And that is how, over the years, we came to incorporate all the lovely words into our trainer-speak. Using words like partnership, choice, release and freedom, and avoiding words like tell, dominate, submission, and so on, will go down a whole lot better with the general public, that's for sure.

But before any of the old style horse folk, who might just by chance be reading this, turn around and say, 'I told you so. You just need to let them know who's boss etc.', that is where I have to say I am in no way advocating or supporting what I consider to be bad horsemanship. I do not condone violence or restraint in horse training, and although I totally admit that I want the horse to do what I ask (or tell) him to do, I also want him to be happy and willing to do it.

Now here's something interesting, right there, at the end of that last paragraph, I could have easily added the words 'for me', and a few years ago I definitely would have. Can you see how that would have made my image and my understanding of horses appear to be a little more friendly. 'I want the horse to be willing and happy to do it for me.' But now, let's be honest here, and again I know we all want to imagine that our horse is doing things 'for us', but he's not, he's truly not. He's doing things because in that moment he feels that it will make him feel better doing it than not doing it, *and that is all.* Get to that point of understanding about horses and suddenly everything becomes a whole lot easier, for both you and the horse.

So now here we are thirty or forty years into the horse being a major part of the leisure industry in modern western society and still we haven't really worked out how things work. On the one hand we have this one bunch of people riding around on untrained animals and the only way they can get the job done is by holding them down with restraints, and on the other hand we have another bunch of people who are desperate to get it right for the horse, but to such an extent that they are tying themselves up in knots with political correctness. And where is the horse in all this? Well, he doesn't want much, he just wants to feel safe, but the first bunch of people are scaring him to death, and funnily enough, so are the second bunch.

Once you get to the point of understanding that the basic primary need of the horse is to feel safe – well, that is a really good place to start. And what does he actually need to feel safe? Well, he needs simplicity and clarity, and he needs to understand what is going on. That doesn't sound too much to ask does it!

But actually this is more about what the horse doesn't need. He really doesn't need a load of human ideas about what they would like him to be or do. Does anyone really believe that horses love jumping – if they did surely they would just pop over the jumps left in the field wouldn't they, or pop over the gate, you know, just for a bit of fun. I'm beginning to think that nearly all of our ideas about horses do in fact come from us looking at them as though they are in fact humans, or at least looking at them as though they think like humans. Well, they don't! Or do our ideas about horses maybe come from our desires for what we would like them to be? Or perhaps even worse than that, do our ideas maybe come from our own need to be wanted, or even to be loved – Ugh!

Again I have to say it. Where is the horse in all this? He just wants to feel safe. He doesn't care tuppence about human stuff – it's got nothing whatsoever to do with him – it doesn't even cause the smallest flicker of interest on his radar. You might want it to, but it doesn't.

If you are still reading this book, and I don't blame you if you are not, please bear with me a little longer – we're almost there. This is simple stuff, and the horse is a simple animal. He just needs to know what it is that you want him to do, and what it is that you don't want him to do. Explain that to him, clearly, and he will be fine. If your ideas about horse training are more complicated than that, then I'd say, have a think about what you are up to, and whether what you are doing is for your benefit or his. Try to keep it simple – your horse will thank you for that!

You know, when I was a teenager searching for some meaning in the universe, a huge part of me didn't want to find an answer. Why not? I think it was because I was enjoying the search so much that I didn't want it to end. It can get a bit like that with horse training, and if you are in that situation then I do think you could rightly say, 'So what does it matter if you want to spend your life trying this and trying that.' Well, I suppose it doesn't really matter, not on a cosmic level anyway. After all it's only horses isn't it. But myself I struggle to keep that sort of perspective. I feel sad for all the horses. In fact it breaks my heart.

Ok, back to the system. You need a horse that is soft and willing to carry out your instructions. You need a horse to understand how to carry you correctly, you need a horse that understands balance, and you need a horse that is straight, or to put that another way, you need a horse that is equally happy and equally able to go both ways, right and left. And all of this is for two reasons. For you, your horse will perform better this way, and for your horse, these things will optimise his physical and mental wellbeing. As the more intelligent partner in the relationship it is our responsibility to educate the horse to be this way.

And so for us, as average everyday horsemen, what is it that we can take from the work of François Baucher and use to our advantage? If you have read this book and you are still thinking that Baucher's work only relates to those people who want to do moves like piaffe, passage, levade etc, then I have clearly failed to make my point to you. Having said that, I do admit that my initial re-action to Baucher was the same. I automatically assumed Baucherism was intertwined with advanced dressage, and to be fair, all those years ago, it was. After all, how do you prove that you are a good horseman? Well, you have to go out there with your horse and do amazing things. And there, right there in that sentence, is where we are so letting the horse down.

There is so much joy to be experienced between man and horse, and truly that joy is not limited to only those of us who can perform majorly impressive stunts. The true joy between man and horse is in the communication, and that is why I wanted to write this book. What I have learned from my fairly rudimentary studies of Baucher's work, has truly transformed my approach to horsemanship. The simplicity it has brought to me, and my horse – well, let's just say, I'm really grateful for that.

In practical terms I have made a start on understanding the importance of the relaxed mouth and the flexions as the starting point for softening the horse. I have begun to understand the importance of balance in all of the horse's movement. And maybe most of all, I have begun to understand the true feel that the horse himself uses in his communication.

Softness, straightness and balance are the keys to the horse feeling good. I know this can easily sound like yet another trite slogan but I hope this little book has helped give some insight into how it can actually be real for even the most average of us who enjoy the company of the horse.

Now I'm off to watch the telly, goodbye!

THE END

A FURTHER CONVERSATION BETWEEN GOD AND THE HORSE

God – Hi there Mr Horse, good to see you. It's got to be 160 years since old Baucher organised that last talk we had.

Horse – Hi Mr God. Yes, I'd say a bit over that actually.

God – Anyway, how's it going? Has much changed for you over that time?

Horse – Oh yes, there have been some really dramatic changes. I'd say mostly in the last sixty or seventy years actually.

God – Right, that's interesting.

Horse – Yeah, we actually had an unbelievable time just under 100 years ago. There was a huge war and millions of us got caught up in that. I'd say that in the entire history of the horse that was probably the most devastating thing we've ever been involved in. Mind you, far more humans than horses lost their lives.

God – Yes, you are right, that was unbelievable. I watched the whole thing with interest, or perhaps it would be more accurate to say, with incredulity.

Horse – What is it with humans that they feel the need to kill each other like that! But anyway, thankfully they have now developed self-propelled machines to take them into battle so we are no longer required. Actually I'd say that since they developed the internal combustion engine round about the beginning of the twentieth century, that's pretty much when things really started to change for us. Over the next fifty years or so, at least in the west, we have been almost phased out as far as transport and work are concerned. Can't say I'm sorry really.

God – So would you say then, that as a species you have more or less retired now.

Horse – Oh no, far from it. We're as busy as ever.

God – Busy! Busy doing what?

Horse – Ha, that's a good question. The humans get us doing all sorts of things. Not sure we actually understand much of what it is we are doing though. Some of it is ok, you know, pretty easy. But some of it is often very confusing.

God – Well, how can it be confusing? Surely they just ask you to do stuff and you just do it don't you.

Horse – Oh my, if only life was that simple. You see the thing is with human beings – they are very complicated creatures. Nothing is simple for them.

God – Yes, I've noticed that too.

Horse – When we worked for our living it was mostly straightforward stuff. At least then, even though we had no idea why, we did at least know roughly what we were supposed to be doing. You know, pull this thing until they tell us to stop, or whatever. Now the tasks that we are asked to do can be very complex indeed. And the way those tasks are explained to us is sometimes just unbelievably complicated. Quite frankly, there seem to be so many theories about how we think and what makes us tick, and so on, and if I'm honest here, not many people really get what it is really like to be a horse.

God – But would you say that on the whole things are getting better for you, or worse?

Horse – Ooooo that's a difficult one. Some things we are put through are absolutely diabolical. I mean take a look at what they call 'top level dressage' for example. Take a look at the way they treat us there. I mean, talk about abuse – it's unbelievable. And then they hand out prizes amongst themselves for reasons that are, quite honestly, unfathomable to us. But then on the other hand there are a huge amount of people really trying hard to get it right for us too.

God – Ah ok, well at least there is some good news then.

Horse – Well, sort of I guess. I'd say the main problem with those people is that even though they are trying hard, most of them have such weird ideas about what horses are.

God – Mmmmm that sounds very familiar. I have that exact same problem with humans too.

A further conversation between God and the horse

Horse – What, you mean that the humans have weird ideas about what you are? I would have thought that what you are is pretty obvious.

God – Oh my, you would be amazed. They have even written huge books about what I am, and then they use those very same books as proof of what I am. It is quite frankly, unbelievable. And sometimes different lots of people, each with their own different books, fight amongst themselves using the books that they have written about me to prove that they are right. I find the whole thing absolutely staggering.

Horse – Oh, now that I am hearing about all your problems I feel like I shouldn't be troubling you with mine.

God – Oh no, don't worry about that. It's not a problem to me. I just keep going, the same as I always do, no matter what goes on. I'm here if anyone needs me. I've always been here and I always will be here. Without me the whole show wouldn't exist anyway.

Horse – Well, that's kind of what I figured. But I do have to say, I think the world would be a better place if people had a bit more respect for what you do and what you are giving them. You know, the way they abuse this planet has to be seen to be believed.

God – Well, I know about that too, and yes, I can see that it could be a bit depressing, but hey, who knows, one day things might improve. But anyway, let's talk about you, not me. Why do you think people don't seem to understand what you are and what you want from life?

Horse – I don't really know. To be honest, we just want a simple life really. And truly, we don't mind having to share our lives with people either – that's been going on a long, long time. In fact, and as you no doubt know, how we are now, all the different shapes and sizes that we come in, well, that's all down to people and the breeding that they have been organising since they first came across us. Yes, basically we're ok with people, and we're ok to work and live with them too. But what we really would like is for them to give up some of their crazy ideas and dreams, and start to see us for what we are. We are creatures who need to feel safe, and we need to understand what is happening. We would, and I think I can talk for the entire equine species here, really, really, more than any other thing, we would like people to find a way of working with us that allows us to feel relaxed and free.

God – Well, that seems to be a reasonable request. Do you think it is actually possible for this to be achieved.

Horse – Oh yes, without a doubt. It can be done. In fact it has been done, and it is being done. It is not actually a complicated thing – it is a simple thing, but as you know, for humans simple isn't always easy.

God – Well, I'll tell you what Mr Horse. It's not my way to interfere in things – I prefer to let life take its course. But just this once, ah now, hang on, I did have a word on your behalf once before didn't I, so I'll just re-phrase that. So I'll tell you what Mr Horse, I'll have another word with Mr Human and see if I can maybe encourage him to improve things for you here on earth.

Horse – Well, Mr God, that would be mighty kind of you to do that for us. Thank you.

God – Do you want me to go into any specifics while I'm having the conversation? It could be tricky. I do know one thing about humans, you have probably noticed it too, they do love making up theories and discovering new ways of doing things. They're not going to be that thrilled if I point out to them that it can all be pretty simple.

Horse – Yep, you're spot on there Mr God. But I think the time is coming where they are just going to have to accept that they are wrong on this one. And actually, if you think about it, the benefits to them of doing the whole thing properly will be enormous. I mean, think how much better we will perform if we are free, and think about how much healthier we will be, and how much longer we will last.

God – Mmmmmm not sure you're right to say they will appreciate that, Mr Horse. There are an awful lot of benefits for an awful lot of people with the situation just as it is right now I'm afraid. There is actually a huge industry built up around the fact that you are struggling with your situation, and that industry isn't going to be too interested in you not having any problems, is it.

Horse – Ah yes, I see your point. It's a bit similar to the way they justify making arms because it creates jobs isn't it. I mean, let's face it Mr God, they're not very bright are they.

God – No, I'm afraid they're not. But hang on in there Mr Horse. They are essentially good at heart and one day I hope that goodness will prevail. Anyway, I'll pop and have a word, and then let's take it from there shall we.

Horse – Thanks God, you're a good egg aren't you!

God – Well, you know, I try to do my best. Bye for now.

RECOMMENDED READING

François Baucher, The man and his methods – Hilda Nelson
This book is an extremely comprehensive collection of literature about Baucher. It is full of stories about Baucher and what equestrian life was like in nineteenth century Paris. It also has translations of lots, if not all, of Baucher's writings, plus some of the writings of his detractors. It also has the translation of the original conversation between God and the horse.

Racinet explains Baucher – Jean Claude Racinet
This book was my introduction to the life and work of François Baucher. I loved it and I have re-read it several times. Racinet was an absolute purist and utterly dedicated to Baucher's methods. The book is extremely easy and enjoyable to read. I would say though, that as to being our first guide to the work, we did find some of the practical advice a little bit mystifying.

Horse Training, Outdoor and High School – E Beudant
This book was published in 1931 so you could say it was written by a modern day Baucherist. It is good to read, and inspiring to get a picture of the simple approach to horsemanship that Captain Beudant takes. I have read somewhere of Captain Beudant being described as the greatest rider that ever lived. When you read about his exploits it's easy to see why.

Twisted Truths of Modern Dressage – Phillipe Karl
This is the book that helped us find the breakthrough we were searching for. The book is packed full of fantastic explanations and fantastic diagrams written and drawn by someone who is clearly a master horseman. We bought this book on the day it was published and from that point on we never looked back. I would say it is a 'must read' for anyone who is interested in seriously studying this subject.